TRAINING CHILDREN
TO BE
STRONG IN SPIRIT

Michael Pearl

Training Children to be Strong in Spirit
Copyright © 2011 by Michael Pearl
ISBN 978-1-61644-037-4
First printing: October 2011

Requests for information should be addressed to:
No Greater Joy Ministries Inc.
1000 Pearl Road, Pleasantville, TN 37033 USA
1-866-292-9936
www.nogreaterjoy.org
mcohen@nogreaterjoy.org

Cover Design: Shoshanna Easling, Audrey Madill

Layout: Elizabeth Aprile, Lynne Hopwood

Illustrations: Debi Pearl, Clint Cearly

Printed in the United States of America

SIX PILLARS

THE SIXTH PILLAR:

TRAINING CHILDREN
TO BE

STRONG
in
SPIRIT

Michael Pearl

Dedication

To our five children and 19 grandchildren and
the 15 more we hope to have -

Be Strong

When God Likes Your Kids

Wouldn't it be great to be able to make simple changes in how you raise your children and thereby put them in the stream of God's special favor and blessing?

It is within your power as a parent to take actions that will bring your children into special favor with God and men. The heart of a Father and Mother can steer their children into a life of abundant joy and prosperity, but most parents have no idea how to make it happen. God says in Hosea 4:6, "My people are destroyed for lack of knowledge: because thou hast rejected knowledge, I will also reject thee, that thou shalt be no priest to me: seeing thou hast forgotten the law of thy God, I will also forget thy children." God will "forget thy children" because of the parents' "lack of knowledge"? What a horrible thought! Where do I get this knowledge?

God clearly favors or likes certain people over others. Noah, Abraham, Ruth, David, Job, Samuel, and Daniel all found special favor with God. We are not talking about God having a warm and fuzzy feeling for them, but treating them in a favorable way—an insider relationship, if you will. Abraham was called "the friend of God." John was "the disciple whom Jesus loved." The other eleven disciples knew he enjoyed that special distinction.

Think of training your children so that in the here and now, and throughout life, they will attract the favor of others. You can do it. This book tells you how.

I am not talking about raising your children to employ gimmicks to "win friends and influence people" so as to satisfy personal ambitions. Jesus "increased in favor with God and man" resulting in his ability to serve God and man—the ultimate work of humanity. The Bible clearly defines six goals of child rearing and reveals practical means for us "to train up a child in the way he should go."

Of the child John, the Bible says:

"And the child grew, and waxed strong in spirit..." (Luke 1:80).

Of Jesus, before he was 12 years old, it says:

"And the child grew, and waxed strong in spirit, filled with wisdom: and the grace of God was upon him" (Luke 2:40).

Of Jesus, after his visit to the temple at 12 years of age, we read:

"And Jesus increased in wisdom and stature, and in favour with God and man" (Luke 2:52).

Of the child Samuel, it is said:

"And the LORD visited Hannah, so that she conceived, and bare three sons and two daughters. And the child Samuel grew before the LORD...and was in favour both with the LORD, and also with men" (1 Samuel 2:21, 26).

Being in favor with God meant that:

"Samuel grew, and the LORD was with him, and did
let none of his words fall to the ground"
(1 Samuel 3:19).

From the Biblical examples we glean the following six pillars of childhood development.

1. *Grew/Increased in Stature*
2. *Waxed Strong in Spirit*
3. *Filled With Wisdom/Increased in Wisdom*
4. *Grace of God Upon Him*
5. *In Favor With God*
6. *In Favor With Men*

Wow! What a marvelous child-rearing plan.

First and most basic, we desire to see our
children grow strong in stature.

Secondly, we desire them to develop
a strong human spirit so as not to
wilt under the responsibilities and
challenges of life—to stand up to
criticism and rejection, to weather
adversity.

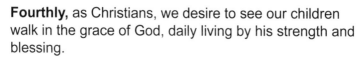

Thirdly, we want to see our children
filled with wisdom and continuing to
increase therein as life demands,
always making wise decisions, never
being foolish or vain.

Fourthly, as Christians, we desire to see our children
walk in the grace of God, daily living by his strength and
blessing.

Fifthly, we want them to gain the favor of God in all things physical and spiritual. To live with God's approval is better than all the riches and power the world has to offer.

Lastly, we want them to become a man or woman that is strong in spirit, filled with wisdom and walking in God's grace, so they will not only curry favor with God but will receive the favor of men as well. With favor from men, opportunities abound for service and a positive influence in the lives of others.

This book is an elaboration of God's six pillars of child rearing.

THE FIRST PILLAR:

Increased in Stature

I. Strong in Body

John "grew and waxed strong in spirit" (Luke 1:80). Likewise Jesus "grew...and increased in stature" (Luke 2:40, 52).

It's easy to overlook the statement that John and Jesus "grew" in "stature". Don't all children grow and increase in stature? Yes, but with varying results. Some are frail and sickly while others are strong and robust. A frail stature harms one's quality of life. Growth troubled by allergies and sicknesses tends toward unhappiness and decreases one's usefulness in the Kingdom of God. Healthiness tends to happiness. Weakness tends to want. Those children raised on quality food, vigorous exercise, fresh air, and plenty of sunshine develop bodies capable of supporting an active life of creativity and service. Constitutionally weak individuals are less capable of performing on every level. Both Jesus and John were destined to much physical hardship and needed strong bodies to support their rigorous ministries.

Jesus expressed disdain for physical and emotional softness when he challenged the Pharisees concerning John's appearance and manner:

"And as they departed, Jesus began to say unto the multitudes concerning John, What went ye out into the wilderness to see? A reed shaken with the wind? But what went ye out for to see? A man clothed in soft raiment? Behold, they that wear soft clothing are in kings' houses" (Matthew 11:7–8).

Jesus commended John's toughness of body and spirit. John was not a frail reed that bent in the wind. He was strong of body and spirit, and did not wear "soft" and delicate clothes. Jesus unfavorably compared the finely

15

dressed religious leaders to the rugged appearance and manner of John, the man who lived in the wilderness, dressed in camel skins, dining on locusts (grasshoppers) and wild honey.

Be Prepared

When my children were growing up, I instinctively felt it important to aid them in developing strong bodies capable of enduring hardship and rebounding in adversity. I wanted them to be strong and agile, capable of saving themselves and others in life threatening situations. I prepared them to run another mile, to climb a rope like other kids climb a ladder, and swim like a Navy SEAL. I wanted them to have the knowledge to build a shelter, start a fire in adverse circumstances, navigate by the sun and stars, gather food in the wild, build traps to catch fish or game, and to use tools and weapons effectively. It is a shame to find yourself in a perilous situation that demands more from your body and mind than it is able. The Boy Scout motto is a good one: "Be prepared." The most basic preparation is a strong body.

To neglect the body is to disparage the temple of God. "What? Know ye not that your body is the temple of the Holy Ghost which is in you, which ye have of God, and ye are not your own? For ye are bought with a price: therefore glorify God in your body, and in your spirit, which are God's" (1 Corinthians 6:19–20). We honor God when we properly develop and maintain the vessel he gave us. Just as I desired the best for my children in education and mental acuity, I knew they needed a body fit for the task of accomplishing all that was in their minds and hearts.

Rebekah, the Indomitable Flower

Our first child was a girl. Rebekah quickly grew into a lovely lady, all girl, but tough as nails. Until she was about twelve we participated in a ministry at a campground called Victory Valley, located north of Memphis, Tennessee. About 40 to 80 young sailors and Marines from the nearby Naval base at Millington spent every Sunday afternoon participating in sports, hiking, boating, and swimming. At the end of the day, we fed them a good meal and then preached the gospel of Jesus Christ. Over a twenty-year period, thousands came to know Jesus Christ and the forgiveness of their sins. Here we are thirty to forty-five years later and from time to time old, bald, fat men drop by to see me and share their testimony of conversion on a Sunday afternoon long ago at Victory Valley Lodge.

To me the great outdoors was definitely better than sports, so each Sunday Rebekah and I took about 20 guys on a hike through the Mississippi River bottoms down to the mile-wide river. It was a hot, humid, nasty environment, filled with mosquitoes, ticks, chiggers, snakes, and lots of mud and slime—a beautiful experience. Rebekah always went with us, as did the boys when they got old enough.

This was during the Vietnam War, so these young recruits would soon be facing guns and terror greater than anything they could imagine. They needed courage, but most were just leaving their boyhood, fresh from mama's table and her scolding for not wearing their raincoats. Every Sunday afternoon I played the role of daddy, sergeant, and preacher.

I encouraged the men to endure the hardships involved in hiking though the swamp by promising them a swim and a rope swing over the mighty Mississippi River at the end of our journey. After about an hour's hard walk through jungle-like foliage, where you couldn't see ten feet in front of you, we would suddenly emerge from the muggy green sea onto the tree-lined sandy bank overlooking the river. They stood gazing up in awe at the sixty-foot high rope swing and the thirty-foot drop to the water below.

It was a pleasure to once again view that awesome river through their city slicker eyes. I never tired of taking these New York sailors and Minnesota Marines on this hike. While they stood along the bank, cautiously looking down into the muddy water, contemplating whether they dare take the swing and the drop, skinny little Rebekah would come whizzing past them on the rope, giving that Rebel yell, her long hair flying behind her like a horse's tail. She would arch into the sky above the treacherous Mississippi and then drop the thirty feet into the murky water below, screaming all the way to the splash. The trigger never failed. The men, as one, would all whoop or utter their Marine grunt and run for the rope. Only about half of them had the strength to maintain a grip on the rope when the G-force increased at the bottom of the swing.

Yeah, I was proud of my little girl. She out-Marined the Marines and out-swam the Swabbies. And if there had been any Air Force there, I would tell you that when she turned loose of the rope she out-flew the fliers.

On our return trip, to get out of the swampy bottoms we had to climb a steep bluff about 100 feet high. It was a 60-degree climb, but there was growth on it that provided handholds. When we all had gathered at the bottom, I would yell something like, "Last one to the top has latrine duty." As one man they accepted the challenge and took off like chipmunks getting out of the road. Saplings were torn out by the roots, vines were dislodged, dirt cascaded down, and grunts, mixed with some swearing, could be heard behind Rebekah and I. Sometimes one of the guys

18

would beat us to the top, but most of the time my young daughter and I stood grinning at the crest to greet the guys as they heaved themselves over the bank to stand on the well-mowed grass above. There we gathered to look back and view the tree tops blanketing the primeval river bottoms from which we had just emerged.

At the end of the day a good meal was served; afterwards the gospel was preached. Many of these men became soldiers of Jesus Christ. If you, the reader, happen to be one of those soldiers back in the 60s, 70s and early 80s, I would love to hear from you. Those were the best of days as my children "grew and increased in stature".

Shoshanna the Swan

When my youngest daughter Shoshanna was about four years old we moved from West Tennessee to Middle Tennessee, where the creeks and rivers were all spring fed, clear, and ice cold. Cane Creek runs right through our 100 acre farm and feeds into the Buffalo River just three miles down the road. The Buffalo has a swimming hole that is second to none just a bike's ride away. There is a rock bluff about twelve feet high with trees leaning over a deep section of the river. In early summer my son Nathan climbed one of the trees and tied a rope to a limb sticking out over the water. It made a beautiful swing. By the middle of the summer all the locals had discovered the swing and gathered every day. One afternoon I took my ten-year-old daughter Shoshanna down for a swim. A crowd of high school boys dominated the rope. Have you ever seen a video-game-playing, macaroni-eating, soda-drinking fifteen-year-old swing on a rope over the river? His little rolls of fat hang from his pink, plump body like plastic bags full of cream cheese. Most of them lost their grip on the rope just as it reached the bottom of the pendulum, never even making it to the G-force on the upswing. They were definitely not growing in strength and stature unless you count the horizontal bulge.

Shoshanna and I waited our turn, but they just passed us by, ignoring our presence. So I asked, "Can my daughter take a swing?"

"Oh no, she couldn't hold on; it would be too much for a girl."

I pressed the issue, but they all agreed it was well beyond the abilities of a little ten-year-old girl. So I just stepped up and took the rope out of the hands of one of the guys and handed it to Shoshanna. But she didn't just swing from the edge of the bluff. As she clung to the rope, I ran up the incline pushing her higher until her starting point was about 10 feet above where the others commenced their swing, and twenty feet further back from the bluff's edge. When she came swinging past the boys, she was holding on with one hand, the other hand on her hip and her feet in a sort of ballerina pose. She swung out to the high point over the river and then rotated her body 160 degrees so she was facing us on her return. She swung past us smiling and relaxed and then made a return trip to the apex over the water where she dropped the thirty feet into the river below, hardly making a splash. The leader of the "Only guys can do it" pack grudgingly said, "Well, I guess she's done that before." Yeah, since she was four years old.

Now Shoshanna and I were not altogether innocent victims of gender and age discrimination. As we left grinning, we knew we were once again accomplices in a big show-off. During the next several days we recounted the experience fifteen times to eager ears ready for a good laugh. Have I ever told you that fathers and daughters that play together stay together—that is, until he can give them away in marriage? And then they come back, bringing their children with them for us to work a little of our training magic on them as well.

Nathan the Tadpole

When the children were very young, before we moved into the country. I constructed a small pond close to our house and stocked it with fish, but it turned out to be the swimming hole as well. The kids were all swimming like frogs—or tadpoles—by the time they were three or four years old. I remember when Nathan was about 18 months old, he could not yet swim, but he was not afraid of the water. The other kids loved to swing on the rope and drop into the water. Though he couldn't take the plunge, he loved to swing on the rope. His sister would hold him up so he could grasp the rope and then let him go. He would swing back and forth over the water several times. When she saw him stop grinning and start straining, she knew he had reached his limit and would catch and remove him from the rope.

One hot summer day three fine ladies, who happened to be friends of my mother-in-law, stopped by for a visit. They were of the cultured sort who never breastfed their babies and put them into preschool. They were fascinated by our "individualistic" life style. As we stood in the shade under the trees talking, one of them screeched, "Oh, help, that baby is swinging over the pond on a rope!" As was my custom, I grinned and patiently explained, "Small children have a much stronger grip than adults and are able to support their weight; he has been doing that all summer and has never…" PLOP! Down he went and disappeared into the murky water. I ran the 100 feet to the pond's edge and dove into the water, baptizing my billfold. He had already surfaced and was trying to paddle his way to shore. When I climbed out with him he was clearly distressed and fearful. I didn't want him to be

21

afraid of the water, so I immediately began to brag about how he was swimming, telling everybody what a tough kid he was. When I saw him grin with self-satisfaction, I walked back over to the rope and put him back on it, letting him swing back over the pond again. But knowing he was distressed, after one swing I took him down and again bragged on his accomplishments. The other kids expressed their pleasure at his daring exploits and within the hour he was demanding his turn on the rope.

I then had to go back and face my three critics. Surprisingly, I suppose because of the outcome, they were all mollified. But I remained a bit embarrassed about my cocky explanation that he would never fall from the rope.

I must warn you; don't follow my example unless you are sure you have complete control of all eventualities. The pond was very small, about the size of a public swimming pool, and the children were never allowed to swim or swing unless we were present. We never had any close calls.

Another Pond Story

That reminds me of another pond story; this one almost cost me my head, as my mother-in-law threatened to knock it off with a frying pan. She was really a sweet soul, just a little overprotective. Nathan and Gabriel are two years apart and were fun to raise. Until they were eight and ten years old most of their friends were men in the military. They knew several Navy SEALs personally. When you get four or five young Marines and Navy guys together they are always competing.

The SEALs talked about their training. One of the things that impressed the boys were stories of them having to learn to swim with their hands tied behind them and their feet tied together. So at five and seven years old

Gabriel and Nathan decided they wanted to give it a try. I made the prospect of them being able to swim while bound more exciting by telling them tales. One they loved was that someday the bad guys would tie them up and throw them off the bridge into the Mississippi River, but it wouldn't bother them, because they would swim out and free themselves.

The training began. First I had them swim with their hands held together behind their backs. In two or three days, they had it mastered. Then I had them hold their feet together and their hands clasped behind them while they swam. Again in a day or two they could swim all the way across the pond in this fashion. The next phase was to tie their hands and feet together with a light string they could break if necessary, but the light string provided assurance that they were indeed following the rules.

Once that got to be routine, I had them jump off the diving board tied up in this fashion, and finally, I threw them off the pier, rotating in the air and landing in odd positions, sinking into the deep brown water. Up they would pop like tadpoles gulping air and off they would swim like porpoises. When they got to the shore, I did not help them. They had to wiggle up on the bank like a salamander and then slide their feet and legs through their tied hands, untie their feet, and then untie their hands with their teeth. Bad to the bone! They loved it and, of course, I did too. Every time one of the guys came over we would put on our little demonstration. The military guys loved the boys as one of their own, and they are still friends with some of them twenty-seven years later.

Outlawed by a Mother-in-law

The boys and I finally learned the meaning of discretion when my mother-in-law came to visit. She was still overprotective, even when the boys were ten and eight years old. I wondered when she would ever let them be men. Yeah, there are some things mothers-in-law and grandmothers just can't handle, but I didn't know it at that stage in my young and inexperienced life. The boys had been looking forward to putting on a show for Nanny, so about five minutes after she arrived I said, "Hey, Nanny, watch this." I grabbed Nathan, the five-year-old, and ran to the pier. I aggressively held him down and tied his hands behind his back and his feet together, and then picked him up over my head and threw him into the pond. I didn't know Nanny could make all those strange noises and say some of the things she said. She was not as sanctified as I had been led to believe. Her protest noises sounded like a cross between the squeal a hog makes when you are trying to load it in a trailer and a marriage counseling session gone badly. I meant for it to be dramatic, but I thought she would have more faith in me than that. Evidently she still had a vivid memory of the tale her city friends told her about Nathan's little splash as a toddler.

Well, that is just one of the lessons I learned growing up. You really haven't grown up until you've learned to accommodate the innate peculiarities of a mother-in-law. Thankfully, that day went better than the time Nathan proved me wrong about the infallible strength of a two year old, for he swam out grinning and then freed himself. That was the first year my mother-in-law failed to give me a new red flannel shirt for Christmas.

Again, I do not recommend you try this unless you have complete control of all the circumstances. If you have foolish sons, you might teach them to do this little stunt, but are they wise enough not to try it on one of their friends when you are not present? In our little pond, the way we conducted it, there was never any danger. We never took risks with their well being.

Both of the boys love water today. Without gear, they can dive deep into the ocean and stay down for more than three minutes. Gabriel free dives deep into the ocean and shoots large fish with a spear gun, hanging on as the fish takes him for a ride. Nathan is a master scuba diver and licensed instructor and he and Gabriel have swum with the pearl divers in the Orient, able to hold their breath underwater longer than the guys who do it for a living.

So, you might be asking, what is so wonderful about your child growing up to outswim pearl divers in Asia? The end was not holding their breath four minutes, but building strong bodies and the confidence that they could handle adverse situations with no harm. And it prepared them physically and mentally for all of life's challenges, even on dry land.

Put to the Test

When Rebekah grew to be a strong young lady, God called her to go to Papua New Guinea as a missionary. After getting her degree in linguistics, she took her brother Gabriel, nineteen at the time, and went to Papua New Guinea. God led them to a tribal chief who had come out of the mountains to shop. He invited them to come to his tribe. They had to fly in a small plane and land on a grass strip on the side of a mountain among the wreckage of other planes that didn't make it, and then spend a day climbing above the clouds. They were the first white people ever to enter the village, but on the word of the chief were well received. They lived in a grass hut on a dirt floor and cooked their rice over a campfire. After about three months, Gabriel left Rebekah alone on the mountain and returned home.

Rebekah had to climb down the mountain a ways to gather water and then carry it up in buckets. She dug ground roots and ate the local diet, experiencing all kinds of diseases and hardships. I remember her stories of being awakened in the night by large spiders dropping from the thatched ceiling onto her bed, and occasionally on her face. They were not poisonous but the fear factor must have been significant.

In her book, *Rebekah's Diary*, she tells of crossing fast moving rivers, hiking down steep muddy mountain trails, crossing giant mud slides on skinny poles imbedded in the mud, while carry a heavy pack. One slip and you would slide hundreds of feet into a logjam at the bottom. On one such trip to another village, she was feverish and weak. The villagers got her home to the village and tended to her until she got well.

She learned enough of the local trade language to communicate the gospel, and in time a family joined her that stayed and taught the people until a strong church was formed. The church went on to evangelize other villages and continues to this day.

Rebekah could not have endured the hardships of this missionary endeavor if she had been weak in body and spirit. It took a tough young lady to hang in there through it all. We raised her to be strong and able. God called her to be faithful. Being ready in body and spirit, she answered the call and bore fruit for the kingdom of God.

Navigating the Swamp

Just last week, my son Nathan, now thirty-two years old and married with four children, was reminiscing about one of the lessons he learned as a small child. We had a secret fishing hole deep in the swamps of the Mississippi River bottoms. It's an old river-run that floods in the spring and is replenished with fish. Cypress trees, ten to fifteen feet in diameter, surround it at water level. You can only get to the back-water lake by traveling across a very flat bottom land thick with hardwood trees five to six feet in diameter which were straight as an arrow, the thick canopy blocking out the sunlight above. The trees are so tall, the squirrels only laugh at you when you try to shoot them out of the top branches with a shotgun. The boys and I loved that old fishing hole. Their grandpa fished there when he was a kid. We always took burlap bags to carry out the fish, leaving when we had caught all we could carry.

On our return trip after a morning of fishing, I would assign one of the boys as the leader of our expedition. When I appointed a boy as the leader, I followed him even if he went the wrong direction and we ended up mired in the swamp, our way blocked by downed trees. He must discover his error and make adjustments accordingly.

As Nathan was recounting his experiences, he told how he would strike out, leading the pack, and every once in a while he would look back at my face to see if he could gather any sign as to whether or not he was going in the right direction. But he said my face was always stony, indifferent to where we were going.

I had taught them to read signs, how to use the sun and the moss on the trees, and to listen for distant sounds. Occasionally, we could hear the faint sound of a tugboat motor on the river about two miles away. The sound needed to be on our right as we made our way out. The moss on the trees needed to be facing us as we headed south. But there were those days when the sun was not shining and the tug boats could not be heard and the moss seemed to have grown all around the trees in the thick, damp timber. When they first started taking turns leading us out, there were occasions when we walked an extra half-mile or so before they got their bearings, but they were always successful in navigating the swamp and forest. On one or two occasions, when I was leading the pack, I had attempted to take a shortcut. Not traveling over familiar territory, I got totally turned around, ending up back were I started; so it was not a "walk in the park" as the saying goes.

Neither the boys nor the girls were ever soft and delicate. They were always wiry and muscular. The process of their physical development was fun for them and terribly entertaining for me. I took great pleasure in the prowess of my children, confident that in a world gone crazy they would survive and be leaders of those who stumble around without hope or direction.

After they became adults, there were times when their physical strength saved their lives or enabled them to endure hardships in foreign lands while engaged in missionary activities. Read *Rebekah's Diary* and you will fully understand.

The greatest benefit of growing strong in body is what it does for the spirit of the child.

No Need to Emulate

Now I know that most of you do not live as close to raw nature as did our family when the kids were growing up. You cannot change your lifestyle to match ours, nor is it necessary. Kids can become strong in body and spirit in a much smaller arena. Country life just makes it the default position, whereas in the city you must schedule events and manipulate the environment to make Navy SEALs out of your five-year-olds. Many families living in large cities have been able to produce children strong in body and spirit. They may be lacking outdoor skills, but their bodies are strong and their spirits are tough, ready for any challenge. In the country, kids have daily chores and responsibilities that impart skill and confidence, but when you turn them loose to do as they please, their bodybuilding and education continues without adult encouragement. Country kids are riding horses, repairing old trucks, swinging on ropes, wrestling, hunting, fishing, running, and swimming all the time. City dwellers have limited options and must use greater wisdom in directing their children into projects that will make them strong in spirit. The back yard should be turned into an exercise and training camp—swimming pool, horizontal bar, trampoline, gymnastic mats, knife throwing and bow shooting range, etc. You can enroll them in classes that teach physical skills, or just provide the tools and let them figure it out.

As a teenager I was raised in downtown Memphis, Tennessee, which is about as low life as they come. My father saw to it that I worked alongside him every Saturday and all summer as a house painter. After public school each day I worked out on the horizontal bar, rode bicycles, and wrestled. But my favorite pastime was exploring the drainage ditches and the empty lots where I found the world of nature. Snakes, small animals, and crawling creatures of every kind became part of my regular collection.

City Slickers

Mel Cohen, who manages No Greater Joy Ministries, is a city slicker from his designer slacks to his barbershop bald head. He is the opposite of me. I have hair all over my head and my wife made the only designer slacks I have. But in a completely different environment, Mel did raise three sons strong in spirit. The boys were raised in a subdivision on the outskirts of Philadelphia. Mel worked in corporate America.

Mel's son Shawn says:

"The main thing I remember about my dad is that he was always there. He always seemed fine with spending hours doing activities that were enjoyable to us as kids. Many nights we did "tickle and fight," which was a mix of him making us laugh by tickling us with just enough roughhousing to make us feel like we were tough. During the summer, Dad would practice baseball with us so that we could be the best possible players on our community teams. I think, because of that special attention, we were perennial all-stars in the little leagues we played in.

Since I have one brother five years older than me and another two years younger, Dad often had challenges getting to our sports games when we were all playing in different little league games. Most of the time when my older brother didn't have a game, Dad would stand between two baseball fields keeping an eye on both my younger brother and me. Otherwise, if we were on the same team, Dad helped with coaching the team.

Remembering all the high and low points of my youth, it was clear that Dad was always available, put his family first, and was consistent in just about every area of his life. He's definitely someone I want to emulate when God gives me a family of my own." Shawn

What Goes Up Must Come Down

When my brother and I were teenagers and living in the city we got into manufacturing explosives to supply the fuel for three stage rockets I built. We launched the rockets in the back yard as all the neighborhood boys came over to watch and to try to help us locate and retrieve the rockets. Sometimes we would find it several blocks away stuck in somebody's yard or lying in the road. As I look back on it I realize how dangerous it was to be standing around looking up in the air waiting for a ten ounce steel projectile to come back down from the clouds, but we grew strong in spirit as we experimented with rocketry.

One time sitting in the kitchen, my mother and I heard an explosion. I knew my brother was in the basement, our workshop, trying to make a more powerful rocket fuel. He was cooking a spoonful of fuel when it went off. Just as we rounded the corner running, he came out with a cloud of black smoke and little burnt spots all over his face and clothes. My daddy was not very understanding; he forbade us from making any more nitroglycerin in the basement.

Lighting Up My Life

My brother also tinkered with electronics and the like. We constructed a gigantic Tesla coil in the basement, directly under the living room. When friends came over, I put on a show. Unknown to them, with the Tesla coil operating in the basement, I entered the living room with a round fluorescent tube in my hand and an electrical cord hanging out of my back pocket. After eliciting a promise of secrecy, and with an air of great mystery, I explained to my friends that I had made a fantastic discovery about my ability to conduct electrical current. Then plugging the cord into the outlet, the other end taped but unseen in my hip pocket, I slowly lifted the circular tube and placed it around my head, putting the two electrical contact points into my mouth. The tube lit up in my mouth as I vibrated and jerked from the powerful flow of current through my body. Actually, I felt nothing. The Tesla coil emits static electricity into the air and everything within six or eight feet of it becomes a conductor capable of lighting the fluorescent tube. My audience never failed to gratify me. They looked fearful, pained, sympathetic, and awed at the same time. I concluded the demonstration by again getting their promise not to tell anyone. Of course they told and when someone came wanting to see it for themselves, I pretended not to know what they were talking about.

My brother also grew up to be strong in spirit, holding seminars on self-defense techniques for women.

Profitable Sports

Many parents are against organized sports, because they recognize you can lose your children to an alien culture. Kids can transfer their loyalties and develop role models that do not represent our Christian values. But sometimes there is no good alternative that provides physical development and healthy competition. Under proper guidance, children can develop a lot of character and grow strong in spirit through participating in sports. The competition, camaraderie, and confidence that are worked into your children through sports can be nearly as effective as the swamps were for my sons. The secret to making it a positive experience is to make it a family event. Daddy must practice with his son and support him with his presence at every game. But never allow the boy to have any reason to think his performance has anything to do with your approval.

A wise parent finds his area of expertise and makes the most of it for his sons' and daughters' sakes. I know of some men that participate in running, biking, or swimming marathons with their sons and daughters. One father I knew took his girls to paintball contests. One of his lovely daughters got to be a consistent winner. They grew up confident and aggressive (and very good shots). Some fathers play golf with their children, even the little guys. Many families camp together regularly, learning and practicing the skills of wilderness survival.

My son-in-law builds motorcycles, and his son Parker, who is not yet two years old, spends a great deal of time "helping" his daddy. When I drop by the shop it is clear that father and son are tying some seriously important strings of fellowship.

My stories come from my experience. What is your experience? Do you have stories? If you don't, it is time to have some fun, to fellowship with your children, and make some memories.

Choosing the Right Place to Drown

Shalom is our fourth child, and is the least bold of all the kids, always cautious. She was never a showoff like her two sisters. She is the practical, dutiful, hard-working servant type. Now grown and married with three children, she also tends to her 86-year-old grandfather, a trying experience most of the time.

Like the other children, by the time Shalom was four years old she could swim, but was scared to get in water over her head. It took us all summer to get her to not fear the water. She has remained cautious in all things.

Last summer, Shalom was at the creek with her three children when a stranger yelled and plunged into the swift, deep current trying to save his ten-year-old daughter who had been swept down the shallow rapids into a deep hole. Neither of them could swim. They were flailing and bobbing, both trying to get back upstream to the gravel bar—an impossible task for the best swimmers. Swimming two miles per hour won't do you any good in a six-mile per hour current. The short story is that Shalom ran to where they were disappearing beneath the surface and dove in, first pulling the girl out of the water downstream and then going back for the father. She didn't hesitate. From the time the kids learned to swim, I had taught them how to save another person from drowning. They practiced on each other.

Shalom is a timid lady, not a risk taker, but she had the body and the spirit of a lifeguard, and she saved a family from a great tragedy that day. She was prepared. She may never need that skill again, but what a shame to face a crisis and stand there shaking in fear, calling for help, wishing you could do something, and knowing you are not equipped. Her life is richer and more satisfying because as a child she grew in stature and continues to maintain a strong body.

In everyone's life there will come an occasion when they are pressed to go beyond the norm. It catches us unawares, it causes us to pause, and then there is an extreme adrenaline rush. Our minds race to find a safe solution, and then we weigh our duty to our abilities. It might be that your own child is trapped in a burning car, or your wife is having a heart attack, but it is your moment to rise to the occasion. Maybe it's an intruder breaking into your home, a fire in the grocery store, an earthquake, or a tornado. Are you physically and emotionally capable of doing the right thing?

Life is a training ground. Some people are trained to look the other way and pretend they are not involved. How will you and your children respond in the day of adversity? Will they be ready to do their duty? "If thou hast run with the footmen, and they have wearied thee, then how canst thou contend with horses? And if in the land of peace, wherein thou trustedst, they wearied thee, then how wilt thou do in the swelling of Jordan?" (Jeremiah 12:5). Are you training your children to have the confidence to walk on the edge to save someone else? It takes a boot camp to produce a soldier. Your home should be life's boot camp. Children strong in body and spirit are not born; they are made one experience at a time.

Down the Well and Up Again

In July, 2011 the news featured a frightening story of a three-year-old boy that broke through the rotting wood covering of an old fashioned hand dug well and plunged into the deep water 40 feet below. When the father and mother rushed to the well, tearing away the rotten wood, they looked down to see their little three-year-old boy treading water and calling "Daddy!" The father attempted to lower a ladder, but it fell apart and proved futile. Meanwhile the boy continued to tread water and call for help. In desperation the father scaled down the rock-lined walls and joined his son in the water, where they waited for the fire department to lower a rope. Both were rescued and the boy went swimming the next day demonstrating an ever-greater boldness in the water.

That couple expressed their thankfulness that they had taught their three-year-old son to swim. Tough daddy; tough son. Strong in body and spirit.

Ready, Willing, and Able

This past year, Middle Tennessee experienced the greatest flood anyone can remember. Shalom's husband's sister, about 30 years of age with three children, was driving her pickup truck down a country road in the driving rain and spotted a car that had gone over the embankment into the rushing current. As she slowed her truck to look, she saw what appeared to be the shadow of a head sticking out of the water filling the interior of the car. Stopping the truck, she hastily ran down the bank, wading and swimming to the nearly submerged car. Looking inside she saw an elderly woman sitting in cold water up to her chin, blankly staring ahead. The door was locked and the woman would not respond. The young woman made her way back to the truck to retrieve a tire iron and a rope. She busted out the window and then tied the rope around the dazed woman and pulled her partially out of the window. Making her way back to the bank, now assisted by a teenage boy, they pulled her out through the window. But the rope slipped off and the now fearful grandmother was helpless in the water. Without hesitation, the young mother dove into the swirling water and grabbed the old lady. The boy on the bank threw the rope to her. She was able to hold the woman with one hand and the rope with the other, the boy pulled them to safety. The woman was taken to a hospital where she recovered and was deeply thankful for a young mother who had the body and spirit to rise to the challenge and save her life.

There is no reason not to raise a hero. Your children don't need supernatural powers. You just need to develop the body and spirit God gave them.

THE SECOND PILLAR:

Waxed Strong in Spirit

1. Strong in Spirit

Of the child John, the Bible says:

"And the child grew, and waxed strong in spirit, and was in the deserts till the day of his shewing unto Israel" (Luke 1:80).

Of Jesus, before he was 12 years old, it says:

"And the child grew, and waxed strong in spirit..." (Luke 2:40).

Strong in Body—Strong in Spirit

We have advocated making an effort to provide circumstances that will enable our children to develop strong bodies, but there is something much more important than physical development—the development of a strong spirit. The experiences that produce physical competency are really just incubators for the development of a strong human spirit.

The United States of America has never seen a generation as weak in spirit as this present one. Progressively, since the fifties, children have grown weaker in body and spirit. I do not want my children or grandchildren to be weak and fearful. I want the boys to have a pair of steel ones and the girls to have the toughness and fortitude of pioneer women.

Soldiers and Sons

As my children were growing up, I was fully aware that the development of their spirits was my number one priority. My familiarity with the training of military men and women may have influenced my thinking. I was aware that the goal of military boot camp is the development of the body; but even more so, its purpose is to strengthen the spirits of the men and women. Airmen, Soldiers, Sailors, and Marines must come to believe in their own abilities if they are to triumph in adversity. They must learn that pain is not a sign to quit; fear is not an occasion to retreat; resistance is not an impenetrable wall, and failure is an opportunity to ready oneself for the coming victory.

Though there is great value in a strong body, those who by nature are frail of body or handicapped are just as capable of developing strong spirits. In reality, it is probably more common to see strength of spirit in a physically handicapped child or adult than in a naturally capable individual. It is fun for kids and parents when children excel physically, but it is even more of a pleasure to see bravery in a child that is crippled, blind, or in some way unable to match his peers. The principle remains the same; push the boundaries of what you perceive as your limits, or what others tell you are your limits, and be an overcomer. Triumph. Achieve. Excel. It is not the heights to which one climbs, but rather how far one climbs above perceived limits that builds a strong spirit.

There are naturally talented or gifted children, performing far above their fellows, who remain weak in spirit, because they have not been called upon to overcome in a wide spectrum of challenges. Again I say, it is not the level of expertise one achieves in relationship to the norm; it is the experience of facing the difficult, the scary, the painful, the boring, and even the impossible and believing in yourself enough to keep trying until you conquer.

This takes place when a ten-month-old conquers walking, when an eighteen-month-old successfully puts his pants on, and a two-year-old gets the courage to jump off the side of the pool into his father's arms. Character is formed and the spirit is strengthened when the five-year-old successfully conducts his daily chores of feeding the animals and gathering the eggs.

When the little four-year-old says, "Look, Daddy, see how strong I am," you need to look and acknowledge his strength, for though physical strength does profit a little, he is at that critical age in life when growth of the spirit is at a peak. If he thinks he is doing well, it is time to brag on his accomplishments. Your encouragement in this area will work wonders.

Blessed are the Poor in Spirit?
(Answering the Critic)

Here I have been advocating making children strong in spirit when Jesus said, "Blessed are the poor in spirit: for theirs is the kingdom of heaven" (Matthew 5:3). I hear some saying, "Shouldn't we strive to be poor in spirit instead of strong? Don't you have to be poor in spirit to get into the kingdom of heaven?" Wow, where do I start? In the first place, the opposite of poor is rich, not strong. And since the Scriptures speak positively of both Jesus and John as growing strong in spirit, it must be a desirable quality.

This passage in Matthew is the only one in the entire Bible that speaks of being poor in spirit. It does have a context that needs to be observed.

It is quite common to hear this passage preached as if being poor in spirit is a desired virtue to which one should aspire, that a poor spirit is a condition for entering the kingdom. I have heard long sermons exhorting us to strive to reduce our self-dependence and humble ourselves in contrition until we are empty of self and suitable vessels for the mercy of God. We are told that the poor in spirit have access to God, while the strong in spirit are shut out. If that is true then Jesus and John were heading in the wrong direction by increasing in strength of spirit. Furthermore, if a poor spirit is a desirable trait then the Apostle Paul and all the other New Testament writers were extremely derelict in not mentioning it even once in all their exhortation to Christians. We cannot name a single apostle that was poor in spirit.

This "poor in spirit" doctrine is a leading tenet of the Amish and Mennonites as well as the Keswick movement. Books like *The Calvary Road* were based on this concept, as well as much of Watchman Nee's writings. This error has caused many to stumble and has wasted precious energy on empty striving to "crucify the old man." It has stifled the growth of many potential leaders. (See my audio series titled *Sin No More*.)

In Matthew 5 the condition of being poor in spirit is a state of need for which the promised kingdom is the cure. Likewise those who mourn or those who are persecuted are promised relief in the kingdom of heaven. And, those who thirst and hunger after righteousness will be filled. Perpetual hunger and lack of fulfillment is not the desired end. Becoming righteous is the end. Mourning is not the goal of a Christian; it is a problem that needs Christ as the cure.

Of course, it is better to be poor in spirit than to be arrogant of spirit, better to hunger after righteousness than to think one's self as righteous, and it is better to mourn for one's lost state than to frivolously frolic in the sewers of sin. It is better to be persecuted for one's righteousness than to find favor with the world by living in conformity to it. For God can address the need of the needy, whereas he cannot feed the full. He came to call sinners to repentance, not the righteous. Though being a sinner qualifies one for God's grace, sinning is not the end; it is the condition of need. Recognition of one's poor spirit is a place of humility and need that can be met in the coming kingdom of heaven.

Since Jesus and John "grew and waxed strong in spirit" I highly recommend it for your children.

John Waxed Strong in Spirit

We see John's strength of spirit in the brief record of his ministry. He went into the wilderness to live, wearing a leather girdle and eating bugs and wild honey—a man of men. He obeyed God in commanding his fellow countrymen to repent of their sins and prepare themselves for the coming Messiah. When wicked king Herod came to gawk, John did not flinch, singling him out and announcing before all, "It is not lawful for you to live with your brother's wife." When the highly respected religious leaders came to observe, he told them to go home and bring forth fruit worthy of repentance. When John was cast into prison, he continued to believe without recanting until they cut his head off and served it on a platter at a dinner party. His blank eyes and open mouth still cried "REPENT" to the crowd of drunk revelers. John was not faint hearted or timid; he was strong in spirit, giving glory to God right up until his death. I want to raise Johns, not Ahabs, who lie in their beds in the middle of the day and turn their faces to the wall whining over their inability to purchase something they can't have.

By the Time They Are Two Years Old

At the moment, Deb and I have 19 grandkids and expect about ten or fifteen more—but not this year. As each grows in stature, I again have the opportunity to do another "clinical" study on child development. It is clear to me that by the time a child reaches his second birthday, his strength of spirit, or the lack thereof, is already quite apparent. The first two years of a child's development are the most critical and telling. If the truth be known, children in the womb are influenced by the emotional state of their mothers.

The way you bend the sapling in its first two years will determine the way the tree leans. It is critical to maintain a positive and creative atmosphere during those first 24 months. Build his confidence and boldness by allowing him to manipulate his environment so as to always be an overcomer. The two-year-old should be a winner in all things. To be a winner, there must be a game, a contest, a trial, and a test of strength or mental exercise.

Confidence is built when a child manipulates objects in his environment. When he successfully drinks from a cup and is praised, when he puts on clothes, picks up after himself, or rides a rolling toy. When a child delights his parents with a page he has colored or a pile of blocks he successfully stacked, he grows in his self-worth. The "can do" spirit is made from many little "I did" experiences. A spirit of "nothing can stop me" grows out of overcoming many little barriers.

Manned Up

I remember a story a lady told about how she manned up her son. She had a loose cover plate on an electrical outlet and asked her four-year-old to fix it. He got a screwdriver, only to discover that a flat-head screwdriver will not work on a Philips-head screw. So he located a screwdriver in the drawer that looked like the screw on the receptacle, and sure enough, it fit. He was elated with his prowess in problem solving. He felt like a real engineer. He fixed the loose plate and placed the screwdrivers back in the drawer. In those ten minutes of success he had grown two years older. For several days, she told everyone they met that her son was taking care of the house, repairing everything broken, for he went around and "tightened" any screw he could find.

Early experiences of this sort will create a strong spirit in your child. To be shoved aside and told that he is not big enough will create a weak spirit that strives for attention in obnoxious ways that only produce more rejection.

Driving Cows and Kubotas

Deb and I took Parker, our 20-month-old grandson, on a ride in our little utility truck. We use it to haul manure and tools around on the farm, as well as kids. Deb asked Parker if he wanted to drive. He jumped out of her lap and stood between my legs grasping the steering wheel just like he knew what he was doing. Driving down the lanes, I showed him how to steer. He already had the general idea from small plastic toys he rode around the house. To our delight he was able to steer with my help, but he kept knocking my hand off the wheel. He wanted full control! So we opened the gate and drove into the 12-acre front pasture. There I gave him full control of the steering. He screamed his delight and triumph, navigating toward the cows. One time he got stuck in a small turn radius and I had to help him straightened it out, but he soon starting steering figure eights around the cows, making them move in protest. He yelled and hollered his triumph until Deb and I were laughing ourselves silly.

At less than two years of age, Parker is already such a man. There is no baby left in him. He wants to do man things, and if his daddy is not around to keep him entertained, he will walk a hundred yards to find me somewhere on the farm working. He loves tools and work. I expect him to be pretty handy in about four years. When his daddy is not working him, I will be. At this age he is already learning the skills from both his daddy and granddaddy.

Being around the grandkids brings to mind the feelings and thoughts I had when my kids were growing up. As I let Parker drive, I knew that I was contributing to his eventual manhood. I was helping his daddy make him strong in spirit. This is something anyone can do!

I do hope my readers can see the principle and spirit behind these personal antidotes. It is not necessary to duplicate my experience; create one of your own. Circumstances and environment are different for each of us. Find the challenges in your environment and participate with your children in fabricating fun in a constructive and rewarding fashion. But don't make the mistake of thinking that board games or iPad manipulation is going to make a child strong in spirit. It takes a hands-on experience in a shifting physical environment to create strength of spirit. Overcoming stress and frustration are essential to developing a strong spirit.

Showing Daddy How to Fish

The first time I took Gabriel, my older son, with me to the backwater lake he was four years old. It was not a park with mowed banks. The heavy growth prevented fishing from the bank. I placed Gabriel about 20 feet from the bank on a log lying in ten inches of water and slime. I didn't expect him to catch anything, maybe a little perch. So I cut a cane pole from the bank and put about four feet of string on it with a hook and no cork or weight. He placed a worm on the hook and walked out to the end of log. As usual, I waded out 50 to 60 feet among the cypress trees and floating logs into water about waist deep. There I had caught crappie and bluegill by the sack full. After I had bagged two or three fish I heard splashing and hollering. Looking around I saw my four year old son off the log, about waist deep in the water, with his torso bowed backward as he strained to hold on to the pole bending nearly double with a large bass running back and forth in the shallow water. He had hooked a four-pounder in the ten inches of water. I didn't even know the bass fishing was any good in the old swamp. I waded to where he was, all the while shouting instructions, "Hold the pole up. Don't let the line go slack. Don't pull too hard. Let him tire out." He had hooked it on a little brim hook. If I had hooked a four-pound bass on a brim hook on a green cane pole in the midst of stumps and submerged logs and limbs, I would never have landed it, but there is something mystical about beginners luck. He landed that bass, and from that day on, he was a bass fisherman in the old swamp. Everybody came to see the bass Gabriel caught. From that day forward, he knew more about fishing than I did to hear him tell it, and he did, over and over again. He still tells it, and he never fails to tack on the end, "And you didn't even know there were any bass in there until I caught that one, did you?"

"No, No, No, I didn't know. You de'man."

Like Father Like Son

In an earlier story, I mentioned Nathan recounting his experience of guiding his brother and I in the Mississippi River bottoms. His mention of it was in the context of sharing a recent experience with his son, who is five years old. Jacob is a bit more shy and timid for his age than his daddy, Nathan, was at five. Jacob is a mild spirited child, gentle and peaceable, very much like my brother the bomb maker was. Jacob has two dominant sisters older than he, and has the temperament of a second born.

Nathan and his family were hiking in the woods when he turned to Jacob and told him that it was now his job to lead the family out of the woods. Timid and reluctant at first, the five-year-old eventually warmed to the task and took his responsibilities seriously, occasionally cautioning the hikers about thorns or dangers, just as his father was accustomed to doing when he was leading. As a symbol of his new role as leader and protector, Nathan gave Jacob a nice pocketknife. He successfully navigated the journey and delivered his charges safely back to camp. They all bragged on his skill, and his sisters were appropriately impressed with his manly abilities.

Nathan said that in the days that followed, Jacob assumed responsibility as protector of the home, keeping his pocketknife close at hand. He now takes it upon himself to go around in the evening and check to make sure all the windows and doors are locked. He handles his knife with great respect, a symbol of his new status. Nathan says, "Jacob perceptibly matured through that one experience."

I am not suggesting that giving your son a pocketknife is going to make a man out of him. He might just cut himself and be afraid of knives the rest of his life. Nor am I suggesting that you need to go on a hike, get lost in the woods, and then turn to your five-year-old to find the way home. He could fail, panic, and thereafter feel like an incompetent coward, forever afraid of the woods.

Before you commit him to a trial, you must be confident that he is prepared and able to overcome. His success is your goal. The last thing you want is to put more on him that he is able to bear. There will come a time when he will be confronted with failure and profit from it, but you must first build his confidence and competence.

Pick It Up and Fix It

My daughter Shalom told how her husband Justin came home bragging about his twenty-month-old son Parker. Justin took Parker to work with him so they could rebuild a 1952 antique metal car, the kind a kid peddles and steers. Justin came in the door declaring, "You just don't know; this is the best kid ever. He is so smart and understands and obeys everything I tell him. He doesn't cry or whine. He is a real man." Now I happen to know that Parker complains and cries a lot when he is at home with his mother and two sisters. He gets downright miserable if he is confined to the house with the women. But if you let him outdoors he will find something made of metal or wood and cheerfully entertain himself all day. He loves tractors, trucks, and tools of any kind.

Justin went on to share how "tough" his son is. He told the story of how Parker was riding his tricycle around in the shop when he turned too sharply and tipped over. He was trapped under the "wreckage" and began to cry for help and sympathy. Justin turned to him and said, "Get up and fix your motorcycle." Justin builds motorcycles and Parker likes to think his tricycle is a motorcycle. Parker was transformed from a helpless, hurt child into a motorcycle repairman. He wiggled out from under his machine and strained with all his might to set it back on its wheels. After several unsuccessful tries he finally got the right leverage and was able to upright it. He then proceeded to examine the wheels and "work" on it until he was satisfied that he had made the necessary repairs. Finally, he stood erect— taller than usual—and grinned his satisfaction at a job well done. His body language was of a celebratory nature—

something between a little jig and a couple jumps. He had triumphed in adversity. He was the man. He had done what daddies do. He fixed the problem.

Now I couldn't make up a better illustration of how to train your boys to be strong in spirit. Justin was training his son to be tough, and when he proved himself tough, he earned his father's praise and admiration—the perfect ground for a father-son relationship.

Can you see the strength of spirit being built into that 20-month-old soul? As the westerners say, Parker will be "a man to ride the river with."

The Little Man

Now I know I have a lot of stories about Parker, but it is because he lives close by and I see him every day. Just yesterday, Deb was watching Justin and Shalom's kids while Mama and Daddy had a night out at the local country diner. I was left at home alone, working on the computer. The door suddenly burst open and Parker was the first one in. As he ran toward me I could see a hasty, concerned look on his face and he was babbling something unintelligible. He walked straight up to me and bent forward, presenting his head and shoulders for examination. Coming through the door Deb explained, "He just got stung by a hornet and wanted to come show you." I could see him puckering up for a cry, so I aggressively said, "Well, little man, you must be tough to take a sting like that. We men can take it, can't we? Yeah, we ought to go kill that hornet. Who does he think he is, stinging Parker?" What was about to turn unto a cry became a look of pride and defiance. He straightened up with resolve and headed back out the door, satisfied that the issue was closed. I asked Deb, "Did he cry when he got stung?" She said, "Yeah, he wailed, but when I tried to show him some sympathy he wanted to come show you."

Responding to him, I remember how I raised my own kids. I instinctively knew that I didn't want them to be crybabies, to be weak in spirit, so I responded to emotional crises as unemotionally as possible, making it an opportunity for them to toughen up and stand their ground against pain and distress. It worked well on my kids, and Parker's mother and daddy have obviously done the same with him. He is a boy that any man would be proud to have as a son. Anyone who looks at that little 20-month-old kid sees the man already budding. Even though he can't talk yet, it is obvious to all that he has a strong spirit.

Building Strength Early

Inner strength is built while developing physical skills. Muscles that are developed before age 25 become a permanent part of one's physique. However, if a thirty-year-old man decides to become a body builder, he can go from fat custard to a muscular man, but when he ceases his rigid exercise he loses all his muscle, returning to a pile of mushy fat. However, when a child or teenager develops a hard body of bone and muscle it remains with him the rest of his life.

As a strong body is best developed in youth, likewise a strong spirit developed in youth becomes a permanent part of the man. I have seen incompetent boys, weak in spirit, go into boot camp and come out playing the man, but in unfamiliar circumstances and unexpected trials they lack the decisiveness and confidence of one who was strong in spirit from a child. The late developer can steel himself and exercise resolve and function with strength of spirit, but it is always a conscious effort for him, whereas those strong in spirit from a child remain strong without effort or thought.

2. Making Children Weak in Spirit

Nature of the Herd

Most parents are clueless. They act as if their children came to them with a guarantee of success—just feed them and love them and everything will work out wonderfully. Not so. "A child left to himself bringeth his mother to shame" (Proverbs 29:15). It is sad to see five- and six-year-olds sent off to the school mill just as they reach that optimum age for growth of the spirit.

Private and religious schools are just as faulty as the public system in one respect. You ask, "What's wrong with corporate education?" It's not the teachers, not the curriculum, not just the morality or the culture, though all that is a problem; it is the inherent nature of a herd.

When children or adults find themselves confined to large groups they establish a pecking order. It is so in the military and in prisons, but much more so in the juvenile classroom. One male child will always rise to the top of the power structure, through superior physical prowess and strength of will. He will employ intimidation and bullying where it is necessary to break others to his will. He will have three or four cronies around him who back up his power plays and bullying. The rest of the kids will "learn their place" in life and will grow weak in spirit, many of them suppressing their natural male drives by resorting to computer games or the like, where they can exercise their wills to autonomous action. Some withdraw into things like Gothic dress and dark arts, where they can be king by means of their secret knowledge and weirdness. The macho clan-leader will not compete with the weirdo on his turf, leaving "eye-shadow, blue haired, nipple-rings" to be supreme in his counter culture.

Properly Socialized

The most common argument against home schooling is "the children won't be properly socialized." By properly socialized they are suggesting that the homeschooled child will not function as well in society. I have never heard a more laughable argument. Don't try to bring that evidence into court. It would be embarrassing trying to prove that public schooled kids are models of social skills and creative independent action. A well socialized public school kid knows his way around drugs, alcohol, and condoms, but he is generally incapable of holding down a job and functioning responsibly. He lacks conversation skills and slaughters the King's English, resorting to "hiphop" language instead.

From what group do you want your children learning their values? What behavior do you want them to emulate: children raised in corporate classrooms surrounded by peers who provide examples of every fault and stupidity the world has to offer, or selected adults who are examples of wisdom and grace? The strength and leadership qualities displayed by most homeschooled children are testimony to the superior socialization of the homeschooled child.

There are exceptions in every category, as the enemies of traditional values love to point out. They can find one in a hundred home school kids that are social misfits, and they can produce one in ten public school kids that are stable and productive. But I say the exceptions confirm our view of public and corporate education.

If you have ignorantly stuck your kid in a corporate classroom and cultivated a little introverted follower with little confidence or boldness of spirit, or a bully that has learned to use other people, it is not too late to make some positive changes.

Survivors of Sodom

I know how upsetting it would be to your lifestyle to take your kids out of corporate education and homeschool them, but it is the best context for producing children that are strong in spirit. It is true that some children will survive corporate education and be very strong in spirit. One of the things that makes them strong in spirit is their battle against the undertow of the contrary culture. I survived public education with a very strong spirit, but I was labeled "antisocial" for my unwillingness to participate in the culture of high school. I was a Christian with strong convictions and viewed the school as my enemy, as Sodom and Gomorrah, something to resist and overcome. My two sisters did not survive the system. It consumed their character and replaced the teachings of the church and home with evil. Many of my church friends, also products of public school, were irreparably ruined by the culture of corruption.

Yes, a few kids will fight the tide and come out as victorious warriors, but the vast majority will wither before the army of Abaddon. The problem for parents is that nine out of ten institutionally educated children will be weak in spirit. Are you willing to roll the dice and trust your kids to those odds? There is an abundance of helpful material on how to get started homeschooling. It is not nearly as difficult as you think. Use your computer to do a search, typing in the word "homeschooling" and the name of your state and county and you will find an abundance of local help to get you started.

A Family Unto Itself

Just as the herd order found in the educational systems has a critically determinate effect upon children's confidence and leadership qualities, similar dynamics can creep into the large family that lives unto itself. If you homeschool in a city lifestyle, all the kids confined in one house and a small yard, individual growth and expression may be sacrificed for the unit. There is no room or opportunity to be different. The confinement produces contention, and one child will rise up to be king while the others must either become happy surfs or rebels.

"That's my chair."

"Tell her to stop singing."

"Don't come in my room."

"Cynthia, tell those boys to get back to their studies."

Pecking order will be established. It may have a girl at the top, or it may be a boy who is power hungry and sees his brothers as challenges to his reign. If your children grow up so confined, you may produce one dominant kid without grace, and the rest of them may lack confidence to act with boldness, just following the herd. Take that same family and put them in a situation where each child has his responsibility to dominate and rule a part of nature, and you are more likely to end up with eight kids that are all emotionally stable leaders—strong in spirit.

All three of my daughters are strong in spirit, but each is different in personality. Shalom is quiet and humble in her leadership traits, but aggressively involved in ministering to others, and Rebekah is philosophical and iron resolved in her commitments, whereas Shoshanna is colorful and entrepreneurial in her leadership traits. Clearly Rebekah has a commanding personality, Shalom has a servant nature, and Shoshanna is the visionary type, but they are all strong in spirit.

Firstborn Sons

It is a widely known and accepted fact that the leaders of nations, corporations, and military commanders are usually firstborn sons. Firstborn sons are naturally thrust into leadership positions by virtue of their age and superior knowledge and strength. You expect the three-year-old to take responsibility for his little brother's safety. The three-year-old shares in the training and instruction of his younger brother. The older brother learns to relate to life as a leader and the younger brother learns to relate as a follower, waiting to be told what to do, expecting to be countermanded in his decisions, and learning to accept it as the way of things.

The firstborn rule is confirmed by the exception. When there are five or more years separating brothers, the younger is likely to be a functional firstborn. Since his brother is too old to be his immediate overseer, the young boy faces responsibilities just as would a firstborn.

Like a firstborn, functional firstborns mainly spend their initial years of life interacting with adults rather than their peers, so the more intelligent and sophisticated members of society socialize them. And when there are five or more years separating a child from his older siblings, he does not have competition, and his brothers and sisters are more likely to relate to him as adults, encouraging instead of competing.

Personality Trait?

Some argue that what we see as a strong spirit is nothing more than an inherited personality trait—some kids will be leaders and others will be followers; their social surroundings will not make any difference. It is true that in any family there will be followers and leaders—no two kids are alike. It is true that in most families one child will be tough as nails and another will be "sensitive." Right from the start, parents must put restraints on some boys to keep them from ruling the world before they are five. Other little guys are not much different from their sisters, especially if they have two or three older sisters and no older brothers. But strength or weakness of spirit has nothing to do with personality types. Weakness of spirit is not a construct of nature, and neither is one's strength of will and purpose. A strong spirit is the accumulation of many experiences beginning at the earliest age, possibly even before birth.

I am the firstborn in my family and my wife tells me that I am definitely the dominant type. My brother, on the other hand, is the mild mannered servant type. Our personalities are opposite colors, but he is just as strong spirited as I am. He even demonstrates leadership qualities, as you would expect from a dominant type. He has always been the employer or manager of other men, having as many as 35 people working for him.

Even when you give birth to a delicate, sensitive boy that seems to be more given to art and music than to swamps and Navy SEALs, there is no reason why he should not grow up to be strong in spirit. Many parents protect the sensitive child and make him weak. All boys should grow up to be all man.

A Warning

We have talked about taking our sons to play ball or encouraging them to get involved in competitive sports, but it is very important for Daddies to not take the competition seriously. It is proper to be deeply satisfied with your child's successes. Their success is your success and a feather in your cap. But be warned. You will do great damage to your children if you take their failure to be a personal affront to your happiness.

Waxed Strong in Spirit

When my boys failed to accomplish the goals they set for themselves or when they could not overcome in a situation I instigated, I knew it was important to be as accepting of them and as supportive as if they had taken first place. I didn't perfectly live my ideals, for I can remember having to manage my spirit sometimes so as to do according to what I should rather than what I felt. It is fine to share your son's disappointment at not achieving his goals, but you should NEVER be disappointed with him when he fails to live up to your goals for him. And you must make sure he always knows he is your number one, no matter his level of achievement.

I am disappointed when I do not win a knife-throwing contest. I threw for several years before taking first place. But I think I enjoyed it more when I was coming up in the ranks, taking third place, then second place. The disappointment of not winning was overcome by the thrill of making a better showing each time, getting closer to the trophy. The day came when I took four first place world championships in one three-day throw, and set a long distance record that has not been broken to this day—hitting a four inch bull's-eye at 63 feet. I did not win the next year or the following. There are some guys that are just better throwers, but I will always know I am a winner, and I continue to practice, hoping to best the best.

My wife and family go along with me to the world championships. They root for me and rejoice when I take first or second or third place, but they never base our relationship on how I do. They share my disappointment, but are never disappointed in me. If any of them ever made me feel that I had to win to hold their admiration, I would slip off to the throw alone and not tell them of it unless I won. Know this, my performance would plummet if I had something to prove when I participated. And I wouldn't want someone in my life that accepted me based on my performance. I would shut them out and find companionship elsewhere, even if they were close family. In light of how I feel—a man 66 years old and very emotionally balanced—can you now understand your son's reaction to your anxiousness when he fails to perform as you wish?

It is not a question of do you love him. The question is, does he know you love him apart from his accomplishments? It is not a question of do you accept your son even in his failure to achieve; it is a question of does he feel accepted by you? The reality is in his perception. What you mean is meaningless. What you intend is irrelevant. The impression you leave is the only impression that matters. And your son and daughter's belief about themselves is entirely your responsibility.

I know. I have been there. You always feel that your sons and daughters are a little foolish, neglect their responsibilities, and are not trying hard enough to reach their potential. They are hard-headed, deceitful, and lazy. You feel the responsibility for their failure and try to prod them to try harder. But they see your zeal and "encouragement" as rejection. I can hear them saying, "He is never satisfied." And later they will say, "He doesn't understand me." In relationships, blame is the knife that cuts the throat little by little. Parents develop an adversarial relationship with their children by communicating that they are not fulfilling their expectations. Add a little anger to the criticism and disappointment and you are using a fifteen-pound sledgehammer to drive a steel wedge between you and your children; and you are guaranteeing they will spend their lives wrestling with their own self-image rather than fighting the big battles that make a positive impact on the kingdom of God.

Every great victory is preceded by failures. Every first place is preceded by many lesser place showings. Every muscle is built with much pain. Don't base your praise and appreciation on their placement at the finish line. Just enjoy your children in the long process of climbing up the ladder of personal development. I don't have the passion for knife throwing that I did when I was trying to reach the top. I can now appreciate other throwers taking first place. I still compete. I am just more relaxed now that I have proven myself to myself. And I never had to prove anything to my friends and family.

How does your son feel about you as a spectator and coach in his journey? Ouch! I feel your pain, but to me your son is more important than you are. Furthermore, you will only become the person you should be when you have nurtured him into becoming the man he can be. Likewise concerning daughters.

3. Leaders and Followers

Society is composed of leaders and followers. It cannot be otherwise.

Followers are essential to the overall good of society. Every engine needs a coal car and a caboose, as every visionary and entrepreneur needs capable, steady men to carry out the vision. But every business needs a manager, and every shift needs a supervisor. Every department needs a head. Henry Ford didn't invent the automobile and he didn't build it. He had the vision, and steady men, working by the hour, built his empire.

There is no loss of personal satisfaction in spending your life fulfilling someone else's vision, but I covet the number one position for my children. I would rather not see them working by the hour, hoping for overtime, fearing a layoff, and concerned as to whether or not they can pay the mortgage. Strong-spirited children grow up believing they can do it better. Strong-spirited individuals are not afraid of failure, for they know that with further effort they will find the path to great success. They keep trying, and they enjoy the struggle.

Nathan Says

When Nathan my son dropped by, I read to him some of what you just read and he shared a couple of observations that will be helpful. Asked why firstborns are the dominant leaders, Nathan explained, "It is easy to give the older kids the responsibilities, because they already have skills and will perform the task much more quickly and efficiently. But that leaves the younger children as observers of life rather than doers. The answer is to take care to put the younger children through the same regiment of responsibility as the older children." That's wise indeed. Learn from anybody you can.

King David, the eighth son of Jesse, was a functional firstborn. He had dominant older brothers, but we find him in the hills alone with the sheep where he successfully defended them against a bear and a lion. As a lad he slew a giant in a duel and went on to be a great general and warrior, a musician, the most quoted poet in all history, and eventually the greatest king of Israel.

On the Farm

It is not necessary for second born sons to grow up with a follower's frame of mind. The one place where I often see several brothers in the same family and all of them confident leaders is on the farm. When I drive by and see my neighbor's seven-year-old driving the tractor, delivering hay to the cows in the pasture, I know he will be strong in spirit. He is given responsibility according to his ability and he fulfills his duty with confidence that he is important in the daily flow of life. He has older brothers, but they are not out there telling him how to do his job. He is the "firstborn" when he is commanding that big tractor and managing a herd of cows. I conclude it is not the order of birth or the personality type one displays early in life that determines the confidence and leadership qualities of a man; it is his early life experiences.

The Overcoming Amish Man

I have told the story before, but it bears repeating here. Years ago, when we first relocated to the country and began to minister to the Amish community, several of the young people felt a call to missions. In preparation, they decided to go to a missions-oriented Bible College located out of state. One young man, about 25, not a firstborn, who had been raised Amish and had about a fifth grade education said he wanted to go to college. When he expressed his interest, I knew I had to talk him out of it. He was not worldly wise. He could read but not well, and had never developed study habits. I didn't want him to be crushed by failure, so I explained how hard it was going to be and what it is like to study for tests night after night, week after week, month after month. He had been raised outdoors, walking behind a matched pair of mules or Belgian plow horses, never confined to books and study halls.

When I suggested he might not be able to make the grade, he looked amused and took on an air of patience as he said, "I can shoe any mule or horse, castrate a full grown bull, fix any motor, repair any farm equipment, and break a wild mustang to pull a buggy. I have never tried anything and failed to do it; I can do this also."

Such ill-placed confidence, I thought. But I was wrong. I had underestimated the power of a strong human spirit. He went to college and took his whole family—wife and kids. He struggled, studying long hours to make Ds his first semester, moved up to Cs his second, and then started making some Bs. He did it because he was "strong in spirit."

John the Baptist was not deterred by unbelief and ridicule because he was strong in spirit. Nor did his spirit fail when he was cast into prison, and it was still strong when they severed his head from his tough body. After John's death, Jesus said that of those born of women there was not a greater prophet than John the Baptist.

The world is an unfriendly place and growing more hostile every day. As your children grow strong bodies, train them to be strong in spirit as well. There may come a day when they will need to be strong in body and spirit.

Remedial Training

When my son Nathan was about eight years old, his aunt invited him over to bring her five-year-old son out of his timidity. Her son had a weak spirit, fearful of venturing into the woods fifty feet from his house. The little fellow was tall for his age, but he grew up in the shadow of his older sister and lacked masculine boldness. So Nathan went over for the day and took along his gear—backpacks, knives, slingshots, BB gun, canteen, etc. He led his cousin out into the "wilds" where they spent the day conquering nature. They discovered and captured various creatures—frogs, turtles, grub worms, beetles, bugs, snakes and the like. They swung on grape vines, climbed trees, and built a "fort," conquering and dominating a two-acre vacant lot. That was the day Cousin became a man. To this day, Cousin is the bold outdoorsman, spending nights deep in river basins hunting, fishing, and coming out in the morning with more food than he can carry. If the world fell into a starvation mode, Cousin would be the man to know. In another day long ago, he would have been called "the food gatherer."

The difference between a child sitting behind an LCD screen and one sitting in the top of a tree waiting for the game to enter "the kill zone" is the difference between a strong spirit of boldness and a weak and timid spirit that lacks confidence.

Strong-Willed?

Many parents defend their stubborn child with the excuse that he is just strong-willed. That parent might interpret what I have said as a confirmation that their child's stubbornness is just a strong spirit. There is a world of difference between stubbornness and a strong spirit. One is evil and the other is godly; one causes those around the child great frustration and the other gives a sense of purpose and order. Do not be deceived in this area. Your child's soul and his life are at stake. Always be honest with yourself for the sake of those you love the most.

4. The Nature of Boys

Dominant Dummies

Just as boys slowly grow into the need to take a wife and build a home, they also grow into the need to control and dominate. It is all part of the process of maturation. You can't have one without the other. God's first command to Adam took into account Adam's nature when he told Adam to "subdue" the earth "and have dominion over" everything on it (Genesis 1:26). Some boys begin to demonstrate their masculine natures in attempting to exercise dominion before they are two. Others don't act much different from the girls until after puberty, but if they are healthy males, there will come a time when parents must make provision for this transition from a child to a dominant man.

If you frustrate a boy's growing need to exercise control and dominance, he will become overbearing and combative, resisting his mother and treating her with little respect. He becomes resentful of her authority as if she were out of place commanding him. If the father is a weak personality and the boy happens to be strong in spirit, as he develops and seeks to assume a leading role, he will have a tendency to judge his father's actions and compete for the leading role. He is trying to fill a vacuum. Understand, the boy does not know he is seeking to usurp authority. He just feels confused, frustrated, and perhaps angry for reasons he does not understand. A king without a kingdom is a loose cannon, an invasion waiting to happen.

If you ignore or frustrate his development, you will lose him, but if you see this growth toward autonomy as a good thing you can direct it into something wholesome and constructive.

Sometime after puberty, usually around fifteen, boys want to be respected. This propensity can have positive results if his mother and sisters honor him and respect him as a man. He will cease in large measure his struggle to prove himself and will relax. But a boy's need for his father's respect cannot be met by anyone but a man. If there is no father or father figure, he is prone to join a gang that has a strong father figure.

Beating the Champ

I can remember wanting to beat my father at arm wrestling. About every three months I would challenge him. The day finally came that I put him down. I was stronger than my daddy! I didn't know it at the time, but my motive was not to prove him weaker, or even to prove that I was stronger, I just wanted him to acknowledge my strength, to recognize my maturity.

As my boys got into their middle teens they were quite skilled in a lot of things. Working in the building trade with other men, they learned a few things I didn't know. I became aware of their anxiousness to have me recognize their abilities, though it sometimes looked like—or felt like—an attempt to put me down. But somehow God gave me the wisdom to see beyond my feelings, so I started asking their advice and deferring to their abilities in certain cases. I could see how much it delighted them and I was aware that it made them like me better. They didn't want a daddy that knew everything; they wanted a daddy that would respect their knowledge and skill. They wanted me to value them the way they valued me. Today they are relaxed advising me, and are very respectful and honoring in their advanced skills and knowledge. I still have the edge on them in a few things, and occasionally make it known. A fellow still has his pride, you know.

I also became aware of their need to communicate the things they were learning from their studies. For fifteen years I was the source of all knowledge. I knew a little about everything and was always relating a tidbit about history, politics, electromagnetic fields, surveying, math, botany, astronomy, zoology, the Bible, and many other things—not that I have extensive knowledge on any of those things besides the Bible. But as they started reading, they gained knowledge I didn't have, even correcting me on points where I was still stuck in the 1950s. I could see their anxiousness to relate their knowledge and be respected for it. I became aware they sought to get the upper hand on me just as I had my father. It was not their goal to make me look like a fool by proving me wrong; they just wanted to be recognized as a worthy intellectual peer. Children can't return respect until you give it to them.

Once they know they are not going to meet any resistance to their attempts at parity, they stop pushing so hard and develop a little humility and grace. But if you fail to communicate your respect, they will push like you were the enemy, creating an adversarial relationship. Wise up, old man.

Girls Too

Girls also experience a hormonal shift when they get into their early teens, but it is not as dangerous as the boys. They don't threaten us with mutiny or anarchy. They just get hurt and grow distant, feeling misunderstood.

Only one of my daughters had a noticeable "crisis," our first child Rebekah. And that was probably because I was still holding on to her like a child, not giving her what she felt was her womanly due. As a child of about thirteen, one day she just pushed away, and within a week or two she was back as a young woman. When I say pushed away, I am speaking of a silent emotional response that most would not have noticed, but it was obvious to me. One day she was a little girl, sitting on daddy's lap, getting hugs and kisses, and a week later she was a young woman with ideas and sensitive feelings that must be respected. It is humorous and glorious at the same time.

Debi the Mentor

When our boys were young, their mother recognized their need to assume their roles as "protectors of the clan". It was a lesson in statesmanship watching her. She was wiser than I regarding this need in the boys, treating them as if she were cultivating them to assume the throne and be her king when they turned twelve years old. Making rulers of them was not of her design; it was their natures to assume the lead. Recognizing the inevitability of it, her goal was to make sure that when their hormones kicked in and they felt the need to take the lead and "rule the kingdom" they would do so with wisdom and grace.

The boys had one older sister and two younger. Just as Deb made it her life's calling to serve me, she organized the girls to serve their brothers—in a limited fashion. She exuded respect for the "men" in the family, and the girls followed her example. There were times when I was just a little embarrassed by her overt commitment to serving us, but she always served.

The deference she and the girls showed to the boys was very constructive, for she assumed that as she served them they would be engaged in fulfilling their duties as providers and protectors. It was understood that the boys would do the heavy lifting, the dirty work, and the tough jobs. They would be outside working in the sun and cold, cutting firewood, tending the garden, repairing the plumbing, and basically securing the life and liberty of the family. The women treated their little "guardians" with respect and deference, because they were earning it. Or was it the other way around? Maybe the boys served, because they were motivated to deserve the special treatment they were receiving.

Reading back over the above two paragraphs, I must confess that it is idealistic. The boys were boys, sometimes complaining about the hard work, wanting to go swimming instead of hoeing the garden. There were plenty of times they were unthankful and took advantage of the girls, and the girls grew irritated at the boys for their bossiness. When you are in the trenches on a hot day in the middle of the summer and the peas need picking or the screen door needs repair, you don't feel like anything glorious or ideal is taking place. If you had been a little bird and dropped by on a hot August afternoon, you might have found Deb nagging me about the screen door and me threatening the boys about getting the peas picked, and they demanding to know why the girls didn't do the picking. The girls might have been dragging their feet about cleaning and washing and cooking, and I might have been complaining about the burnt beans we had for lunch. I confess this reality, because I do not want you to be discouraged after reading this. But, from the overview, the trend was always upward. The "idealistic" philosophy I express was a trend that produced fruit in the long term.

Have you ever looked at a ten-year chart of the price of gold? If you go back ten years, it looks like a fairly straight line with a constant incline. Values rose seven hundred percent. But if you look at a monthly chart, and especially a daily chart, the line jumps up and down like it was going nowhere. Raising your sons and daughters is a fifteen- to eighteen-year process. There will be ups and downs, but we want the ups to be much higher than the downs, so that ten years from now the chart will show significant upward progress toward raising up sons and daughters with strong spirits, filled with wisdom and the grace of God.

The frailty of human flesh will create a drag on our idealism, but "Keep thy heart with all diligence; for out of it are the issues of life" (Proverbs 4:23).

Practice your ideals and hold onto them, even when the opposite seems to be the reality, and depend on the mercy and grace of God to make up the difference. "And let us not be weary in well doing: for in due season we shall reap, if we faint not" (Galatians 6:9). Truth and love have a way of winning in the end. To me our family was special, but I know we were ordinary Christians, living and learning as we went along. We didn't start out wise, and we were not always in control as if we knew exactly what we were doing. We lived each day as it came and expected tomorrow to be even better. In the end our gardening bore beautiful fruit, and for that we give glory to the God of mercy and grace.

V. Fat and Folly

Grasshoppers and Honey

John and Jesus "grew" and "increased in stature."

Logically, a discussion of diet should have been first, under "Growing In Stature", but I didn't want to lose my reader with a most unpopular subject—eating right to live right.

I am not going to try to teach you the facts concerning the dangers of the American diet. There is a flood of material available that you have already either read and acted upon or chosen to ignore. But knowing what I now know, if I were starting my family all over again, there would be no sugar, no vegetable oils, and no processed foods in our diet. That's the big three evils. If you cut those out of your family's diet, your family won't suffer from the sicknesses and diseases so common to all. When I say no sugar I am also talking about things containing sugar, like catsup, salad dressings, crackers, cereals, fruit juices, bread, as well as the more obvious sweet treats.

Fat and Food

Both John and Jesus grew in stature. Can you picture a fat Jesus or a plump John? Everybody expects their prophets to be skinny. A fat person is an undisciplined person—weak in spirit. The world is filled with temptations of the flesh, food being the most universal test of our personal discipline. One of the primary Christian traits is temperance. A person intemperate in any area is intemperate. If one lacks the discipline to control his mouth, how can he control any other member of his body? Wow! That was politically incorrect.

75

It is sad to view modern, overindulged children with their soft squishy flesh and muscleless bodies. They whine and complain while moving from chair to couch. As I said earlier, muscles and strength of bone developed before age 25 will remain with you the rest of your life. The earlier you build muscles the more permanent they are. The sixteen-year-old boy that is a tough woven chord of muscle and sinew will retain that physical stature for the remainder of his life. If he later adopts a sedimentary lifestyle, he may grow fat, but the muscle structure underneath the rolls is apparent, and with a little dieting and exercise he can recover his early strength and stature.

Likewise, a soft, pudgy kid who grows up and then decides to change his lifestyle, adopting a proper diet and exercise program, can get rid of his fat and develop some muscle, but six months after ceasing his regiment he will return to the same pile of mashed potatoes he was before—all muscle gone.

The same holds true for girls. A fat little four-year-old is a prophecy of a fat forty-year-old mama. Children who are fat during their developing years create larger fat cells and establish a standard to which their bodies default. Their norm will be fat for the remainder of their lives. It takes much more effort for them to maintain muscle and a proper weight.

Parents just don't realize what they are doing to their children when they provide a diet that makes their children overweight. The harm is permanent.

Practical Truths

Anyone who has ever butchered an overweight chicken has seen the great blobs of fat that crowd the internal organs, choking the life from the animal. It is scary to think this happens to people as well, and these inner blobs of fat are hard to lose with dieting. Allowing your child to be overweight is deciding their lifetime fate. It is putting a lifetime curse on your child, making diseases come on him much sooner and more severely.

Being overweight limits what a person can do, who they can marry, and how they feel about themselves as well as how others feel about them. And in addition, every day of being overweight is a day of cultivating a weak spirit. Every year of overweight, starting with the toddler, is a permanent enlargement of the fat cells, leaving them with a lifelong struggle to maintain a healthy weight. Don't start whining about positive affirmation and the need to be positive toward a fat child. Fat is not genetic and it is not an unavoidable disability. It is the result of choices made and habits formed. Parents need to face up to the fact that fat is not just a matter of appearance; it is an undeniable issue of health and the ability to function at normal levels.

We are being told that this is the first generation that will bury their children. Parents are feeding their children to death. Are you killing your child with too much food or with junk food? Are you causing your child to lose out on the blessing of being in favor with man?

A Poor Man's Health Plan

Organic is wonderful, but it is not usually available to most of us. Range-fed meat and barnyard chicken eggs are God's food. Raw milk and cheese taken from range-fed beef that has not been medicated is food from the Promised Land. Remember, John the Baptist did not eat processed food or strained and cooked honey. His grasshoppers were range-fed and his honey still had bee legs in it. But, thankfully, there are not that many grasshoppers in my area. Legs in the honey I can handle.

Homemade whole wheat bread made from non-genetically altered grains and homemade noodles are the staff of life, and home grown and preserved vegetables are down home goodness, but very few of us are in a position to manage our diets so well. To eat so, you must either be rich and have it delivered to your home daily, or you must be poor from the production of it. A poor man living on a small farm, with not much additional responsibility, can dedicate the biggest part of his day producing quality food for the family. And even he will have winter months and early spring days with little fresh food available. At such times it is tempting to eat store bought macaroni-and-cheese or purchase a frozen pizza. I have succumbed.

But, if you are not a successful homesteader you are not helpless; just cut out all sugars, processed foods, and vegetable oils, and you will improve the health of your children by 80 percent. The specialized organic vegetables and range-fed meats, eggs, and milk will raise you another 20 percent, but eliminating the big three evils will be hard enough and will produce tremendous rewards.

There is no need for children to have allergies and asthma, no reason to have decayed teeth, unless, of course, they drink fluoridated water and use fluoridated toothpaste. There is no reason for your teenage daughters and sons to have terrible acne, constipation, allergies, and constant colds. A healthy diet is achievable. It will allow your children to grow and increase in stature as did John the Baptist and Jesus. Do your own study. Your children deserve it.

How Do I Get Kids to Eat Vegetables?

I am often asked how one can get his children to eat vegetables and all the healthy things. I admit, most everything that really tastes good is bad for you. It takes effort to acquire a taste for healthy food, but once you experience the sharpness of mind and lightness of body that comes with healthy eating, when you try to eat some of the delicious junk you feel like a stopped up sewer line and it encourages you to stick with the good stuff.

If you have allowed your children to eat cereals and processed foods, it will be difficult to break them of the habit. When serving white beans and chicken-bone soup with fresh sliced tomatoes and cucumbers in vinegar they will think you are torturing them. They will refuse to eat or eat so little that they will be hungry in one hour and will be prowling the cabinets where the processed food is waiting to jump out and consume their health. The solution is an easy one. Not painless, but quite simple.

The secret to changing our diet is at the grocery store. Do not buy and bring into your home anything that contains sugars or corn syrups. Nothing with vegetable oils; in short, nothing processed. It's simple. When there is nothing in the house to eat other than things that are good for you, they will learn to eat it and, in time, like it.

The problem, dear parent, is not the kids; it's your addictions. You want them to be healthy, but are not willing to pay the price. You are willing to buy healthy food and "try" it, but you are not willing to cut the bridges behind you and purge your home of all processed foods, sugars, and vegetable oils.

You are like an alcoholic that wants to quit, but keeps a bottle just in case. There will always be a "just in case" event until there is no bottle available. Cold turkey is the only way to go. I assure you, the first three months of giving up all junk will give you the feeling that your throat has been cut and your stomach is eating your backbone. If you don't feel like a martyr you are sneaking around eating poison. When you have gone without sugar, vegetable oils, and processed foods so long that you begin to feel superior to your weaker fellow men, you know you have mastered the flesh, if not the spirit.

Now, you will make the transition much easier if you get some cookbooks on healthy eating. You can purchase several good ones from www.BulkHerbStore.com. I have watched families try to eat healthy and they just about starved to death and died of boredom. If you just drop the junk from your diet, there will be nothing left to eat except bland vegetables and meat. An experienced cook, or a woman with good recipe books, can dress up zucchini, squash, and green beans, turning them into tasty delights. Most women have never learned to cook, because everything comes ready to heat and serve. It will take your family several months to a year to make a transition to pleasant, healthy eating. But it's worth it.

Religious Eaters

Some people have such a weakness and addiction that they must be "religious" about a change in diet. They are constantly on the verge of "falling off the wagon," so they cannot tolerate a single violation of the rules. They are hard to be around—complete Pharisees, bigots, and boneheads. They look over your shoulder and scold you for not eating as they do. I have been on both ends of it, so I know what I am talking about. But once you get the family adjusted to healthy eating, you can break the rules and eat junk every once in a while without ill effect. Junk food will always be a temptation, because the devil is in the cake. They even named one after him. The secret to maintaining your discipline is to never bring junk home and put it in the cabinet. Occasionally the family can go out for pizza or hamburgers and have a carnival (fleshly indulgence), and it will be a great treat. Just make sure you routinely eat to live, not live to eat.

THE THIRD PILLAR:

Increased in Wisdom

Increased in Wisdom

The Bible provides us with an amazing outline for rearing our children.

The Bible says of the child Jesus before he was 12 years old, "And the child grew, and waxed strong in spirit, filled with wisdom: and the grace of God was upon him." (Luke 2:40) And again we read after his visit to the temple at age 12, "And Jesus increased in wisdom and stature, and in favour with God and man." (Luke 2:52)

From the Biblical examples we glean the following 6 phases of childhood development.

1. *Grew/Increased in Stature*
2. *Waxed Strong in Spirit*
3. *Filled With Wisdom/Increased in Wisdom*
4. *Grace of God Upon Him*
5. *In Favor With God*
6. *In Favor With Men*

In the first chapter we covered growing and increasing in stature. In chapter two we covered growing strong in spirit. We will now discuss being filled with wisdom and increasing therein.

I. Growing in Wisdom

Before age 12, Jesus was "filled with wisdom." After his visit to the temple we are told that he "increased in wisdom," indicating that he developed wisdom incrementally. Jesus learned wisdom from life's experiences and from his study of the Word of God. No doubt Mary and Joseph aided Jesus in his increasing wisdom, as did his community and the local synagogue. At age twelve, when he visited the temple in Jerusalem, he was found asking questions of the learned men. He was still growing in wisdom, as well as sharing some of his own.

The Absence of Wisdom

There was a frightful phrase I heard occasionally when growing up—"Foolish boy." It was uttered with a shake of the head and downward pitch in the voice, a tone somewhere between disgust and sadness, as if someone had died. When my parents or my dear grandmother pronounced that denunciation upon a boy, I knew he was being dismissed as the most unworthy waste of fried potatoes and pork chops the community ever produced. A "foolish boy" was stupid, irresponsible, had poor judgment, and was not to be trusted or befriended. I can still hear the unreserved exhortation, "Don't keep company with fools." At the time I didn't fully understand the implications of their judgments, but by the time I turned seventeen or eighteen, I began to see the negative fruit of those "foolish boys." They died in car accidents while driving too fast, or they got some girl pregnant, flunked out of school, were arrested, or got hurt in fights. All developed reputations as worthless. "Fools die for want of wisdom" (Proverbs 10:21).

Thank God for Wise Fathers

When I was five years old my father attended a revival meeting at the newly formed Baptist church about a mile down the country road from our little farm. He and two or three of his brothers and sisters heard the gospel of Jesus Christ and were born again. From that day forward we never missed a single meeting at that one-room church house.

At least once each year I heard a sermon on how King Solomon had asked God for wisdom. The preacher always brought the story to life, describing the event wherein God gave Solomon a choice; he could have anything he wanted just for the asking. My imagination ran to the things I would ask for if given one wish.

Wisdom was not one of them. Riches, complete victory over his enemies, power, and long life—Wow! How could one ever decide? And, why did Solomon choose wisdom? I learned that he became the wisest man who ever lived, writing many proverbs. This knowledge began to work in me the desire to seek God for wisdom; the seeking changed the whole course of my life.

I was fascinated with the wisdom by which Solomon determined the rightful mother of a baby. Two women who had just given birth, perhaps at a midwife's house, slept in the same room with their babies, and during the night one baby died. They both claimed the living infant as their own. They were brought before Solomon to settle the dispute. One woman was lying, but how would anyone determine the true mother? "Cut the child in half and give each woman part of the child,"

Solomon commanded. "Yes, cut it in half," one of the women cried.

"No!" screamed the other, "She can have the baby."

Then Solomon said, "Give the baby to the woman that is willing to give it up to save its life; she is the real mother." So that is wisdom, I mused as a child, not fully understanding how wise that decision was.

Without wisdom Solomon would not have been able to decide correctly in the many great issues that came before a king. The preacher, Howard Vickers, told us to ask God for wisdom. Why not? If it was good enough for Solomon, it must be good enough for me. So, as a small child, still not fully understanding why I should prefer wisdom to wealth, I started asking God for that elusive virtue—wisdom.

Teen in Need of Wisdom

In time, as I grew into my teens and the specter of making life altering decisions was before me, I began to see that wisdom was an invaluable gift. How will I know whom to marry? I need wisdom. How will I decide my vocation in life? Where will I live? What should I believe in regard to differing Biblical doctrines? Which church is the right one? How should I raise my children when I get married? Should I send them to pubic school? Should I go to college? Which one? What should I major in?

By the time I got into my later teens, I coveted wisdom, seeing it as the most important quality I could possess. I prayed for wisdom every day. What if I married the wrong girl? What if I went to the wrong college and met the wrong people and was taught the wrong subjects and influenced in the wrong direction? What if I chose the wrong occupation and lived in the wrong city and drove the wrong car down the wrong road at the wrong time? "God, please give me wisdom. Show me the way and guide my path. Don't let me do something stupid." At 66 years of age, there is a prayer I still pray every day, sometimes several times a day: "Lord, save us from foolishness; give us wisdom."

"If any of you lack wisdom, let him ask of God, that giveth to all men liberally, and upbraideth not; and it shall be given him" (James 1:5).

I never feel wise, but I always feel the need for wisdom from above. Solomon said, "Trust in the LORD with all thine heart; And lean not unto thine own understanding. In all thy ways acknowledge him, And he shall direct thy paths. Be not wise in thine own eyes…" (Proverbs 3:5–7). I never take wisdom for granted, for here I am half a century later and yet I know I can still be a "foolish boy."

The word "wisdom" appears in the Holy Bible 234 times.

The book of Proverbs contains the word "wisdom" 54 times.

Solomon's Ecclesiastes uses the word "wisdom" 28 times.

A Sampling of the Word Wisdom:

"Get wisdom, get understanding: forget it not; neither decline from the words of my mouth.

"Forsake her not, and she shall preserve thee: love her, and she shall keep thee.

"Wisdom is the principal thing; therefore get wisdom: and with all thy getting get understanding" (Proverbs 4:5).

"How much better is it to get wisdom than gold! and to get understanding rather to be chosen than silver!" (Proverbs 16:16)

Increased in Wisdom

"For the LORD giveth wisdom: out of his mouth cometh knowledge and understanding" (Proverbs 2:6).

"Happy is the man that findeth wisdom, and the man that getteth understanding" (Proverbs 3:13).

"He that getteth wisdom loveth his own soul: he that keepeth understanding shall find good" (Proverbs 19:8).

"Whoso loveth wisdom rejoiceth his father..." (Proverbs 29:3).

"The rod and reproof give wisdom: but a child left to himself bringeth his mother to shame" (Proverbs 29:15).

"Then I saw that wisdom excelleth folly, as far as light excelleth darkness. (Ecclesiastes 2:13)

"The wise man's eyes are in his head; but the fool walketh in darkness..." (Ecclesiastes 2:14)

"For wisdom is a defense, and money is a defense: but the excellency of knowledge is, that wisdom giveth life to them that have it" (Ecclesiastes 7:12).

"Who is as the wise man? and who knoweth the interpretation of a thing? a man's wisdom maketh his face to shine, and the boldness of his face shall be changed" (Ecclesiastes 8:1).

"The fear of the LORD is the beginning of wisdom: a good understanding have all they that do his commandments: his praise endureth for ever" (Psalm 111:10).

"But of him are ye in Christ Jesus, who of God is made unto us wisdom, and righteousness, and sanctification, and redemption:

"That, according as it is written, He that glorieth, let him glory in the Lord" (1 Corinthians 1:30–31).

"If any of you lack wisdom, let him ask of God, that giveth to all men liberally, and upbraideth not; and it shall be given him" (James 1:5).

"But the wisdom that is from above is first pure, then peaceable, gentle, and easy to be intreated, full of mercy and good fruits, without partiality, and without hypocrisy" (James 3:17).

Jesus Grew and Increased in Wisdom

"Wisdom is the principal thing; therefore get wisdom: and with all thy getting get understanding" (Proverbs 4:7).

As my children were growing up, I did give great attention to their developing strong bodies and spirits, but I possessed an even greater passion for them to become wise. Wisdom is the ability to discern between options and make the best of all choices. Life is a stream of alternative paths, some leading to destruction and ruin, others to honor and a good name. The road we travel is seldom marked as good or bad. Most choices do not contain great fault and are acceptable to the general public, but many small unwise choices will result in great error. I heard a powerful statement when still a child, "Others may; you cannot." The wise path is sometimes the lonely path.

Wisdom is something akin to the gift of foreknowledge. It requires the heart to see the end and choose accordingly. Only great integrity and principle can guide the mind in knowing the end and selecting the righteous path.

Wisdom is alien to fallen humanity. An appetite for pleasure and pride governs us. The wise path is more often one of self-denial, where pleasure must be delayed or denied altogether. To choose according to truth instead of expediency is wisdom. One must know what is right and value it for reasons higher than the self, if he is to make wise choices on a daily basis.

When I took my children into the Mississippi River bottoms to fish, I was always concerned that they should avoid getting bit by a Cottonmouth Moccasin snake, but that risk never seemed as perilous as the possibility that they could grow up to be just another one of the world's fools. Wisdom is an inoculation against the serpent's bite both in the swamps and in society's sewers.

Even small children need wisdom. It is never too early to begin "growing in wisdom." A mother hen is desperate to teach her newly hatched chicks a bit of barnyard wisdom essential to their survival. I have watched a hen warn her chicks of danger. The other hens and the roosters are a threat to young chicks, for they will readily kill a little one that gets in their way when feeding. So the mother hen will snatch her chicks up and fling them on the far side of her body when another hen approaches. She teaches them to be wise in their food gathering, to guard against other barnyard animals and naughty little boys.

One day a hawk killed one of the chickens, and for several days the hen kept her chicks under an outbuilding where they could not be seen from the sky. She kept an eye in the sky for the deadly predator and taught her little ones to flee under cover when that ominous shadow appears on the ground. A dumb cluck will be hawk chuck when it runs out of luck, but a wise bird will still be heard crowing in the morning.

If a hen left her chicks to their own devices, they would never survive their first few weeks. It is so much more important that we parents communicate wisdom to our little ones.

Discerning Good and Evil

The Bible speaks of children as having "no knowledge between good and evil" (Deuteronomy 1:39). As a child, Jesus learned to "refuse the evil, and choose the good" (Isaiah 7:14-16). Our children come to us as blank pages that must be filled. We write the early pages of their life's story, laying the groundwork that will determine how their lives will play out. "Train up a child in the way he should go: and when he is old, he will not depart from it" (Proverbs 22:6). A child without training is a child without wisdom—a victim or victimizer in the making.

Every day of your child's life will be a time of deciding what is good and what is evil. His perspective on the good and evil will either be in keeping with truth, thus rendering him wise, or it will be warped and skewed by the world, leaving him somewhere between slightly unwise and a stupid fool. The world is populated with stupid, inept pleasure seekers and lazy bums. It is the default position, the destiny of unregenerate humanity. Only radical intervention on the part of parents can produce a wise child that will grow up to be a wise adult. Thankfully the public schools are so ineffective that about 10% of the students escape the fool's label.

Four-year-old Wisdom

There are those occasions when our children impress us with their maturity. I vividly remember one such occasion. When our first child, Rebekah, was just four years old, I met another artist, a sculptor, at a show in which I was displaying my art. I invited him and his wife to come stay with us for a couple days. They also had a four-year-old daughter. Our motive for inviting them for a visit was to share the gospel, which we did rather constantly. On the first morning, as we were sitting around the kitchen table talking I could hear Rebekah and the other four-year-old talking in the bedroom about ten feet away. Their voices got more passionate and aggressive. Rebekah was "contending for the faith," extolling the virtues of Christ and the need to believe upon him. Even more amazing was that the other little girl sounded like a confirmed infidel, heatedly denying that Jesus was God and contending that he should not be worshiped. There has probably never been an occasion when I was more surprised by children. The contrast between the two was amazing. Being our first child, my experience with children was limited, but to this day I have never seen anything like it. The intensity and singular passion of the two was a display of eternal light and terminal darkness. From that point on, I began to take children much more seriously, knowing that if we as parents give up those first four years we have forfeited the most formative years of their lives. Rebekah demonstrated strength of spirit and wisdom I didn't know was possible in a four-year-old.

Fire and Folly

I have a friend whose six-year-old son climbed up in the barn loft and lit a candle. His parents would have forbidden him from doing it, but there was never an occasion to teach him this lesson. On that horrid day they were gone and their twenty-year-old daughter was watching the children. She was in the house, not knowing that her foolish little brother was sitting in a pile of hay with a burning candle. She heard the screams and rushed out to the barn, which was already shooting flames into the air. She climbed to her brother and, with his clothes still on fire, she carried him out of the flames. She was burned on her arms and one side of her face. The little fellow was burnt over 95% of his body. He lives today and does his artwork with a brush held between his two fingerless nubs. He is a brave young man who worships God and has nothing but thankfulness in his heart, but he and his family have gone through unimaginable suffering because he made one unwise choice. Much wisdom is garnered through life-altering mistakes. Bringing such events to the mind of your children, and asking them what could have been done to avoid this tragedy, can help build wisdom in their souls and minds.

I know the parents of this young man must wonder if they could have done something that would have prevented this tragedy. It is natural to do so. But what's done is done. They must make the best of the road they walk. I am sure they would have some advice for us; they would warn us to instruct our children to consider their ways and exercise wisdom.

Old Folly

When I was sixty-four years old, I was working on my house, and was very frustrated that I couldn't get any help. I rigged a scaffolding and tried to hoist a 4x8 sheet of Advantech, which is heavier than plywood, up over my head to place it on the roof. It was a foolish decision, employing a foolish technique that resulted in about eight breaks to my wrist, arm, and shoulder. It took me seven months to completely recover, feeling stupid the whole time. When I try to go through a metal detector they call for backup. There is something about two metal plates and eleven screws that make the machines scream "Stupid, Stupid".

Increased in Wisdom

When Deb and I first got married, we lived close to her parents. I often helped her dad on the farm. I delivered calves, picked up hay, and mended fences. He taught me how to operate a tractor and implements, how to fabricate metal and weld, and many other things I never learned growing up. He called me "Meathead," rather unaffectionately I might add, and occasionally told me, with expletives, that I would never amount to anything.

I learned much from him. He was always warning me against the dangers inherent in any chore we were undertaking. He had survived two ship sinkings in the Second World War and survived repeated trips driving a landing craft on D-day. He had worked at Dupont, where he had seen several of his friends die when they failed to follow the rules. He was extremely safety conscious, and imparted that caution to me.

As my kids came along I found myself following in his tradition. No, I never called them Meathead, but I did teach them safety. From the time they could understand language, I was always warning them of possible dangers. I didn't just tell them; I showed them. I remember setting up a demonstration of how easily a gas can will explode. I showed them how quickly loose, dry hay will burst into flames, how sawdust or grain dust in the air will explode if exposed to open flames or a spark. I warned them against playing with sharp sticks and wire, and running amidst dangerous debris.

I constantly told them that they were responsible for the safety of others. If one of the children did something that caused another child to get hurt, I gave the offender a good spanking to reinforce my admonition.

Bicycle Bully

One time when Gabe was about 30 months old, a twelve-year-old second cousin who lived just down the lane rode his bicycle over Gabe as he was walking in our driveway. The kid often made sweeping passes close to the other kids, but this time he accidentally got too close. He claimed that Gabe stepped out in front of him, and his daddy assured us it was just an accident. The boy was not wise, and neither was his father, for his son grew up to be a fall-down tragedy. If one of my children had demonstrated carelessness with his bicycle and had run over another child, I would have spanked him firmly and then not allowed him to ride a bicycle for six months. If children are going to grow up to be wise in the use of an automobile, they must learn wisdom in the use of a bicycle.

Circus Stunts

When the kids were small, one of the boys constructed a see-saw type board like you see in the circus where someone stands on one end while another person of greater weight jumps on the other end, propelling the first one into the air fifteen or twenty feet. One of the boys put his little sister on the flying end and jumped on the other, propelling her into the air two or three feet so as to come down landing on her head and shoulder. Not seriously hurt but shaken, she did what little sisters do best: she screamed bloody murder. I am sure the boy did not mean to hurt his sister, but he was definitely unwise, so after expressing my shock that he would be so careless, I gave him ten good licks with a switch cut from a willow tree. I am confident that the moment he saw his sister flying through the air like a shot quail, he knew his destiny was with the willow tree and not with the circus.

Developing Wisdom

It is a pleasure to watch the grandkids developing wisdom. When I see a five-year-old taking responsibility for her two-year-old brother or cousin, making sure he is safe and doesn't come to harm, I know I am seeing something godly. When there are four little kids jumping on the trampoline and a two-year-old loses his balance and piles up in the middle between six jumping feet, bouncing and tumbling uncontrollably, complaining mightily, and the kids stop immediately to come to the rescue of the little one, I know I am seeing the budding of wisdom based in compassion.

Gun Safety

I had taught my boys gun safety and allowed them to go in the woods alone with a gun. I never allowed them to handle a gun with others present. It is nearly impossible for a kid to shoot himself with a gun that is as long as he is tall, but most ten-year-olds are not old enough to be trusted with a loaded gun where others are within range—except on a gun range where he is closely guarded. Gabe was ten years old when he brought home his first deer, killed with a .22 rifle while squirrel hunting.

Through much admonition and example, I taught my boys to handle a gun safely. I told them to imagine that inside every gun, sitting behind the trigger, was a little demon with his foot on the firing mechanism just waiting for the gun to swing past another person so he could shoot them. So a gun was never—never—never to be allowed to point at another person, not even for a split second. Never swing the barrel past anyone.

There is no better tool to teach a kid gun safety than having his own BB gun—the low powered kind that only pumps one time. When they turned about five I allowed them to buy their first BB gun. I explained to them how it could put out an eye or break the skin, and I told them that they would be allowed to have a shotgun when they learned to handle the BB gun carefully. I warned, "If I ever see the BB gun swing past another person I will take it away from you for six months." I remember, on at least one occasion, taking the gun away from one of the boys for what seemed to him a lifetime—six months. They learned gun wisdom and are most careful today.

A Deadly Lack of Wisdom

When my boys were about twelve and ten years old, they had an eleven-year-old second cousin who lived just down the road from us. The boy's father bought his son a short-barreled .22 rifle—too short for a kid. At the time I mentioned to the father that the rifle was an unsafe choice for a young child. I also talked to my sons about the gun and why it could be a danger to their young cousin. One day the guys all got together for a skeet shoot. They lined up to take a shot at the clay pigeons as they were flung out over a dry pond. My boys and I showed up to join the excitement. As soon as we arrived I watched everyone to make sure all were going to be safe. After getting ready to fire and then failing to do so, the eleven-year-old cousin lowered his shotgun to hip level, parallel with the ground and swung around to face the crowd. I saw the gun was cocked and the boy's finger was on the trigger. He had swung the barrel past ten people. I immediately took charge of the weapon and warned everyone of the danger. The whole crowd of men and sons looked amused at my alarm. When they brushed the boy's carelessness off as if it was of no consequence and allowed him to continue to handle the gun, I knew it was time for us to leave. It was clear to me that the incident was not only dangerous, but it would also work the opposite of caution and wisdom into all the young boys watching. We got out of there like our pants were on fire.

As we walked home, I took the occasion to again explain the extreme danger that had just occurred. Six months later the young cousin was out alone with his short-barreled .22 rife. While climbing a muddy bank he shot himself through the lungs and heart. The imprints left in the mud showed that he was using the stock of the gun for a walking stick, which left the barrel about waist high. His father found his son hanging in a barbed wire fence he had tried to cross just after being shot. The daddy hurriedly carried his son home. I arrived at the house just as he died. It was a horror I will never forget, one of the saddest days of my life. I can only imagine the grief of the boy's father, losing his son in such a tragic manner.

The accident was the result of what had been in the making for several years. There was a chronic lack of wisdom all the way around. Wisdom is given for many things, including our safety.

A parent must be alert and take charge when there is danger. Sometimes you have to make a scene, even judging others, but you cannot let the feelings of others prevent you from exercising all caution. The devil, the world, and even good-meaning friends can sometimes steal wisdom from your sons and daughters, wisdom you strive so hard to instill. That day at the shoot, when the other men smiled in mockery at my alarm, was one of those occasions. If at that time I did not have my sons' hearts and respect, then my own boys might have judged me as silly and overreacting. Thankfully my sons had reason to trust my judgment and wisdom. At the funeral of their young friend, I am sure they remembered the day when I made a scene fleeing from the folly of friends.

There were many times after the boy's death that I referred to this incident as a basis of reminding my children of the importance of handling a gun safely. It was a negative lesson in wisdom, both for little boys with guns and fathers who are responsible for them. I am sure that today my thirty-five-year-old son, who was about the same age as his young friend who died, is still guided into paths of wisdom by the negative example of that day.

Making wise decisions affects every area of a child's life. We have already discussed how overeating can destroy a child's life. Fat brings on a lingering death where the gun causes instant death, but both spring from a lack of wisdom.

II. Teaching Wisdom

Jeremiah

My five-year-old grandson Jeremiah can discuss the value of choosing healthy foods like a professional dietary doctor. When he visits, he often reminds me to make wise choices in my food intake. This knowledge of healthy living will follow him all his life. Gaining knowledge and self-restraint with food translates into all areas of self-discipline. Jeremiah has more self-discipline than most adults. I am thankful to say that all 19 of my grandchildren have lean, muscular bodies, the result of good choices in eating and play.

A parent can only give what they have. If you lack wisdom then now is the time to start asking God for the wisdom to train your children. If you lack knowledge then you need to stop wasting time on useless entertainment and busy yourself in studying health, safety, and practical sciences.

Window of Opportunity

Parents have a unique window of opportunity to teach wisdom in regard to personal habits. The first four or five years of a child's life are a dispensation of near total dependence and trust. They have not yet learned to question your decisions—unless you train them to. There is that brief time when you can be their will and their self-discipline. You can set the boundaries, and you can easily constrain them to choose the path of patient self-denial. In the early years of training they are not actually choosing to deny themselves. It is through your control of their environment that you can arrange many opportunities for them to experience deferred gratification in a manner that instills habits in the will. They will see two options and their flesh will want to indulge, but you choose the path of self-denial, and they experience the feelings of not doing what the carnal self would do. You are exercising their wills to make the hard choices of self-denial. Under your management, their souls triumph over their bodies and they develop strong spirits and bodies that yield to the will. As they get older and are put in a position to make independent choices, they have already mastered the essence of self-denial and are accustomed to the feelings of not seeking instant gratification. It is like learning to live with hunger instead of sneaking food from your neighbor's garden. It takes practice. The desire to be gratified is common to all children and adults. The difference between us is that some are wise enough to say no, whereas others are fools for believing that their carnal choices will not produce greater misery in the end.

Five-year-old Wisdom

Admonition and spanking do not impart wise habits. Habits are earned one choice and one action at a time. Bad habits come quickly, but good habits are formed through many positive choices. The problem with children is that their knowledge of good and evil is so undeveloped that they cannot make well-informed decisions. Furthermore, when children have never been trained to practice caution or self-denial in any area, it is impossible for them to suddenly be noble in denying their flesh. It takes maturity, which children don't naturally possess, to say no to the pleasure road and to take the narrow path of deferred gratification.

There are only a few people who will ever hand their son a loaded gun like the unwise father, but most people reading this book will be guilty of overindulging their children with junk food. Death comes in brass bullets and cellophane wrappers. Death by spoon can bring more frustration and suffering for children than unwise parents are prepared to endure. Wisdom to make small choices in learning self-denial is critical for a happy, healthy, productive life.

Just the other day, Jeremiah my food guru grandson came into the house alone. Deb had just made some ice cream out of homemade yogurt and honey. She makes sure I maintain wise habits by not making it very often. It was a hot day and Jeremiah looked like he would appreciate something cold, so I offered him some. "No," he said, "I can't have any sugars or milk products right now."

"Why not?" I asked.

"'Cause Mama thinks I may have an allergy."

"Well, what about a peach, can you eat that?"

"No, no fruit either." I must admit that I was amazed. He didn't bemoan his restrictions. He didn't sneak a bite. He was highly self-disciplined. I don't think Shoshanna was that disciplined when she was five, but she has taught Jeremiah self-denial. It is now a habit. He wisely assumes that life is built on denying gratification for a greater good. He doesn't have an ounce of extra fat on his muscled little body.

How do you teach a child to be wise and self disciplined? For one thing, Shoshanna and James have discussed the science of nutrition and the human body with their son. He grew up thinking of food as a tool to an end greater than self-indulgence. He actually understands the connection between what you eat and how your body functions. He is wise in the ways of diet and health and is therefore able to make informed decisions.

But even before Jeremiah was old enough to understand anything, his parents placed limits on themselves and on him. He was taught to be moderate by their enforced boundaries. In his flesh, he developed the function of self-denial before he could reason and choose.

A Positive NO

The key word is "NO." Learn to say "no" to your child. I am not talking about a harsh, threatening no. I am speaking of the act of discrimination. Not all things are equal. Not all opportunities are beneficial. The disciplined life has more nos in it than yesses. When you walk into a store, everything in there begs to go home with you. There are many things we would like to have, but we walk down the aisles silently saying, "No, No, No" and finally, "Well, possibly just one new shirt would fit my budget and not be overly extravagant." Life is a million options with only a few wise possibilities.

When Johnny wants to eat "now," cause him to wait another ten minutes until you get it on the table. When he is pushy about junk food, if it is something you intend to allow him to have, cause him to wait for a while so as to deny instant gratification. When you go into a store and he wants you to buy him something, don't do it. Explain that it costs money and daddy has to work hard for money, and the child doesn't really need it. If a child is demanding in a store, expecting you to indulge him, then you must never buy him anything until he has learned to be happy doing without.

When a child becomes passionate about any indulgence, consumed with the need, and you give over to his demands, you prevent him from developing wisdom and self-discipline.

Organize your life so that your children grow in discernment and wisdom rather than in indulgence. Know for certain that wisdom and runaway indulgences are mutually exclusive.

Wisdom Through Observation

The most immediate way to learn anything is through experience. But who wants to learn car safety by having a wreck? So the next best way to learn is by observing the experience of others. I took every opportunity to direct my kids' attention to the tragedies and just plain foolishness around us.

I hardly ever went anywhere without at least one of the kids going with me. When we were in Memphis and spotted a drunk lying in the gutter, I began to tell an imaginary story as to what led to his demise. I told about his first drink, thinking it was cool, how the other kids dared him and he gave in to them. I told them that he never intended to become a drunk, but the alcohol in one's blood takes away the will to resist. Every drunk they saw was one more page of wisdom to be remembered.

In those days we were doing a lot of ministry with hippies and street people. The kids heard the testimonies of converted drunks, dope heads, fornicators, jailbirds, prostitutes, homosexuals, murderers, and thieves. When the guys and gals dropped by the house with desperate needs, the children saw the aftermath of poor choices. When some of the "converts" fell back into sin, the kids saw the power of old habits. They heard the weeping confessions when the prodigals repented again. My children grew in wisdom with every negative example.

When they came home with a tale about a cousin or an acquaintance at church that did something or said something inappropriate, I used it as an opportunity to warn them of the dire consequences that resulted from such actions. I explained how anger or lust or greed would destroy their lives and steal their virtue. They understood fully the consequences of sin and it made them wise.

When we met a lazy family living in poverty, dependent on government or charity to survive, I again took the opportunity to teach the kids how laziness will bring you to ruin and to dependence on the government or others. They saw it. They understood the need to be diligent in work.

When friends or relatives had bad attitudes, expressing anger or bitterness, I again used it as an illustration of the evils of an undisciplined spirit.

As they were growing up, with a little encouragement and interpretation of the facts from Deb and I, they saw the evils of selfishness destroy families and ruin reputations. Cousins they played with when they were young, cousins that were already demonstrating a propensity to walk a crooked path, have grown up to create a life of misery and ruin. My kids were there as witnesses. It was a school in wisdom. Even an evil man would fear and hate sin if he were made to observe the consequences of it for fifteen years before he had the opportunity to walk the same path.

Developing Wisdom From the Word of God

The best source of wisdom is the Word of God. I am not saying this because this is a religious book and needs the credibility of showing deference to church teachings. I am speaking practically, not theoretically, when I say the most effective way to learn wisdom is through frequent exposure to Bible stories.

"The entrance of thy words giveth light; it giveth understanding unto the simple" (Psalm 119:130).

"Study to shew thyself approved unto God, a workman that needeth not to be ashamed, rightly dividing the word of truth" (2 Timothy 2:15).

"Now all these things happened unto them for ensamples: and they are written for our admonition, upon whom the ends of the world are come" (1 Corinthians 10:11).

Personal Testimony

When my father came to know God through Jesus Christ it changed his life. I was only four at the time, but my earliest memories were of my parents reading to me from a Bible storybook. I can still remember the tiny little illustrations at the beginning of each chapter. Now, sixty plus years later, I can duplicate the drawings from my memory. I remember the feel of the newsprint paper and the texture of the brown cover. It had diagonal lines running both directions across the cover, and a dark brown spine. Even today when you mention a Bible story like David and Goliath or Samson or Daniel in the lions' den, my first thoughts are of the things I learned when I was four, five, and six years old. I looked forward to the evenings, because I knew one of my parents would be reading another exciting story.

As my brother and two sisters came along after me they also learned their first Bible stories from that ragged book. It eventually fell apart, but we kept the pages in order as we again read it from cover to cover. I last saw it when I was in my late teens. I don't know what became of the paper and cardboard, but the stories live on in me. I would give a hundred dollars for it today. It seemed like a magical book. Through its pages I came to know God.

I can also remember the Bible stories told by the preachers and Sunday school teachers. Later I read the stories for myself and discovered additional truths. I didn't realize it at the time, but I was not just learning about Daniel and his faith; I was learning about a covenant keeping God who does what he says he is going to do and is faithful to his people.

Early in life I developed a God-centered worldview. I cannot remember ever seeing the world other than as the testing ground for fallen humanity, as a battle between good and evil, a place where men take one side or the other and pay the consequences for their decision. At the earliest age I knew the wages of sin is death and that God sees and knows all. I knew there is a judgment day coming and we will all give an answer for every deed. I believed in reaping and sowing. "Be sure your sins will find you out." (Numbers 32:23) "Be not deceived; God is not mocked: for whatsoever a man soweth, that shall he also reap. For he that soweth to his flesh shall of the flesh reap corruption; but he that soweth to the Spirit shall of the Spirit reap life everlasting. And let us not be weary in well doing: for in due season we shall reap, if we faint not" (Galatians 6:7–9).

I also learned and firmly believe that God does indeed bless his own, and there is peace and joy for those whom he favors. I wanted to be on God's side. All this I learned as a small child through Bible stories, and it molded my young life.

When I was thirteen and fourteen years old and was tempted to sin, I always knew I was under the watchful eye of a God who sees and records every deed. Let me tell you, that makes a difference in a young boy's life. The world of a fourteen-year-old going to public school is filled with conflicting choices—very few good. It was the Word of God hidden in my heart that made me wiser than my peers. "Thy word have I hid in mine heart, that I might not sin against thee" (Psalm 119:11).

How to Teach Wisdom

You teach children wisdom like you teach everything else: line upon line, here a little and there a little.

"Whom shall he teach knowledge? and whom shall he make to understand doctrine? them that are weaned from the milk, and drawn from the breasts. For precept must be upon precept, precept upon precept; line upon line, line upon line; here a little, and there a little" (Isaiah 28:9–10).

Notice the repetition. It is constructed so as to illustrate the repetitiveness required in teaching children. Child training is not a single pill you administer; it is a way of life. Teaching is not one event, nor many events; it is an uninterrupted stream of relating to your children. I say again, "More is caught than taught." If parents live wisdom and relate to their children in wisdom, then admonition will be readily understood and well received.

You will want to teach them the Bible stories, not skipping the horrid parts, for then you must make application in all of life's events. Call their attention to both wise and unwise actions by everyone around them. When they do something really stupid, ask them if it was wise, and then discuss it, considering how they could have made a wiser choice. Lead them in praying for wisdom, and cause them to understand "that wisdom giveth life to them that have it" (Ecclesiastes 7:12).

The Real Thing

It is helpful to use bright colored Bible storybooks to teach the four and five-year-olds, but you should also teach directly from the Bible. Do not use the short, watered down, childish Bible storybooks. If they purge the story of hard realities, leave the books on the store shelf. If the pictures are realistic, they can be used as visual aids, but you will want to use the Bible to get the real storyline across. You will want them to form an association between the pleasure they experience when hearing the stories and the open Bible. Their curiosity should be piqued at the mysteries within that precious book.

When I think of my long-departed grandmother, I see her open Bible lying on the bed with her wire rim glasses on top. Long before I could read, I was curious as to why she spent so much time reading the Bible. When my father started reading Bible stories to me, I understood, but the mystery of her commitment to that worn book remained with me. When I came into her little one-room house and interrupted her Bible reading, I felt I had suspended something sacred.

I also have memories of my father studying his Bible, as he sat next to the dresser in our one room house. A kerosene lamp sitting close to the mirror reflected twice the light, enabling him to continue reading as I went to sleep close by. One night the mirror got too hot and cracked. At the time, it seemed like a big thing.

Our life centered around the Word of God and participation in church meetings—Sunday mornings and Sunday nights, and Wednesday night prayer meetings (we prayed), Thursday night visitation and evangelism, four eight-day-long revival meetings each year, missionary week, Vacation Bible School, special speakers, choir practice, special music programs, and then dinner on the grounds.

Like everyone else around us, we were poor in the world's goods, but rich in the Word of God. I was raised on a King James Bible and Christian example. As I got older I realized our family was different from our neighbors and acquaintances. We were Christians and lived by a different light.

Gabriel Learns to Read

Our first son Gabriel seemed to get a slow start academically. He was quite bright and showed a curiosity to learn many things, conquering math quickly, but he was just not interested in reading. It was an indoor thing and he was an outdoor person. Before he was five years old, Deb had schooled him in phonics and done all the things preparatory to reading, but he was just not interested, and we didn't push. By the time he was eight years old, we were beginning to get concerned. Then one day he walked in from outside, laid down his BB gun, took his knives off, and announced to his Mother, "I want to learn to read the Bible like Daddy." He had sat though many a Bible study and had listened as Deb or I read to them from the Bible and he heard me discussing the Bible with others, and had now decided it was a tool he needed. He didn't care anything about reading itself. He just wanted to be able to access the content of the Bible.

Deb immediately dropped what she was doing and opened a King James Bible to Genesis 1:1. She read it slowly, pointing to the words, and had him repeat each one, continuing every day, several times a day for about two weeks, and he was reading on his own. He already possessed the fundamentals of reading, but he had no reason to read until he felt a need to personally access the words of God.

Oral Reading Skills

As the children were growing up, at least once a week we had oral reading practice. Each child stood behind a makeshift podium on the far side of a big room and read from the Bible. The object was to teach them to read in public with boldness. It also taught them self-confidence. I corrected them on enunciation and diction, requiring them to keep their chin up and occasionally look at their audience, projecting their voices and reading with conviction. We laughed a lot, and everyone was relaxed and enjoyed it. Even the little ones who would "read" a book with the words upside down were included in the "reading." They would sit in Deb's lap and as she slowly read the words, pointing to each, they would repeat them.

The kids never attended (on a regular basis) a church where the preacher invented his sermons. The only thing they knew was expository Bible teaching. Growing up, they heard every Bible story more than once and could tell you about the woman Jael, who drove a tent stake through a sleeping man's head. They knew about the bears eating the little children who mocked the prophet. They could tell you about the things David suffered because of his sin and the blessings of God on Daniel who obeyed the Word of God.

Occasionally we still sing, "The B-I-B-L-E, yes that's the book for me; I stand alone on the Word of God, the B-I-B-L-E."

My children are all grown and are into their late twenties to late thirties. All five are married and have several children, more on the way. They have made and continue to make wise life choices. The Word of God is central in their homes just as it was when they were pointing at words and pronouncing them after Mama.

THE FOURTH PILLAR:

Grace of God Upon Him

The Grace of God Was Upon Him

First we covered the subject of children growing and increasing in stature. Then we dealt with growing strong in spirit, after which we discussed growing in wisdom. We will now consider "the grace of God was upon him."

I. Greatest Gift

There is not a greater gift from God, not a greater blessing this life has to offer, than to have the grace of God upon us. If God were to grant just one request to every Christian father, surely all would choose that the grace of God be upon their children. If I were cast upon this planet, left to my own resources, facing the certainty of my eventual demise, and given the nature of sin and death, my one request would be that the grace of God be upon me.

If I lived in a big city full of crime, as they are, and had to commute across town every day on busy interstates, and work in a high rise building, I would covet the grace of God upon me.

About 4000 years ago God reviewed earth's inhabitants and decided the human race was an affront to his holiness, an insult to his dominion. He was sorry he made man upon the earth and would remedy the situation by killing every soul by means of a great flood. But then the Bible text says, "But Noah found grace in the eyes of the Lord" (Genesis 6:8). That grace was an act of provision. God gave Noah the plans for building a survival box, one in which he and his family would float above the floodwaters. The grace that Noah received was not a spiritual experience; it was objective assistance.

What Is Grace?

What is this grace that was upon Jesus Christ as a child? Certainly it had nothing to do with God having mercy upon him, for the sinless Son of God did not need mercy. Nor is this grace a personal virtue as we might speak of one who is graceful. The New Testament speaks much of grace as a gift from God that enables us to live the Christian life. "Let us therefore come boldly unto the throne of grace, that we may obtain mercy, and find grace to help in time of need" (Hebrews 4:16). Mercy and grace are different. Mercy is God's willingness to forbear the punishment we deserve. Grace is the provision of God "to help in time of need". Christ needed no mercy, but he did need the daily favor of the Father. So we are told that the child Jesus had the grace of God upon him. The last verse in the Bible is John's prayer for all believers: "The grace of our Lord Jesus Christ be with you all" (Revelation 22:21).

Ruth, An Example of Grace

Ruth was a widow from a foreign country who followed her Hebrew mother-in-law back to Israel after the death of her husband. She was a poor foreigner in a strange land and was reduced to picking up the leftovers in the fields after the harvest was complete. Boaz, a wealthy landowner in the lineage of Christ, had many people working for him. Ruth inquired about gleaning in his fields and Boaz said, "Go not to glean in another field, neither go from hence, but abide here fast by my maidens: Let thine eyes be on the field that they do reap, and go thou after them: have I not charged the young men that they shall not touch thee? and when thou art athirst, go unto the vessels, and drink of that which the young men have drawn" (Ruth 2:8–9). To his generous offer and his guaranteed protection, Ruth "fell on her face, and bowed herself to the ground, and said unto him, Why have I found grace in thine eyes, that thou shouldest take knowledge of me, seeing I am a stranger?" (Ruth 2:10).

Ruth characterized his "taking knowledge" of her as an issuance of grace. It was not mercy she received; it was favor accompanied with provision.

Boaz carried it further: "And Boaz said unto her, At mealtime come thou hither, and eat of the bread, and dip thy morsel in the vinegar. And she sat beside the reapers: and he reached her parched corn, and she did eat, and was sufficed, and left. And when she was risen up to glean, Boaz commanded his young men, saying, Let her glean even among the sheaves, and reproach her not: And let fall also some of the handfuls of purpose for her, and leave them, that she may glean them, and rebuke her not. So she gleaned in the field until even, and beat out that she had gleaned: and it was about an ephah of barley" (Ruth 2:14–17).

Handfuls Of Purpose

Through Boaz's express favor, Ruth had gleaned about a half bushel, about 33 liters—enough to make bread for her and her mother-in-law for a month, and that was in just one day. At that rate she would glean a year's worth of bread in just 12 days. In addition he offered her the opportunity to share meals with his own workers and a safe place to sleep during the night. He eventually made her his bride, which placed her into the lineage of Christ. Ruth is a beautiful picture of needy Gentiles receiving the grace of God and becoming Christ's bride.

From Ruth's use of the word grace we can better understand the concept of raising children with "the grace of God upon" them. It can be said that God's grace is upon one in whom God delights and makes full provision for his daily needs.

Another Example of Grace

Peter writes to husbands concerning the grace that is so essential to daily life: "Likewise, ye husbands, dwell with them according to knowledge, giving honour unto the wife, as unto the weaker vessel, and as being heirs together of the grace of life; that your prayers be not hindered" (1 Peter 3:7).

When a husband has knowledge that his wife is a weaker vessel and gives honor to her, she receives grace from him and the two of them are "heirs together of the grace of life." Now that's profound. We receive grace to assist us in our daily lives. The grace of life is God's moment-by-moment favor and blessing. It is life-enhancement from on high.

The Boy With Grace Upon Him

Jesus grew up with God "taking knowledge" of him as Boaz did of Ruth. Jesus received delivering grace, as did Noah. Jesus remained in fellowship with the Father, and in his weakness, God poured assisting grace upon his son. When the time came for Jesus to suffer as the sacrificial lamb, he retreated to a garden to pray, and there he received suffering and dying grace. The Bible says he "endured the cross," because the grace of God was upon him from a child.

How could we raise children in this ungodly world without the grace of God upon them? Would Noah have survived the flood without the grace of God? Ruth would have starved without the grace of Boaz, and a wife would be miserable without the grace of her husband. Let us raise our children in the grace of God.

The Source of Grace

Parents are not the source of grace. Certainly we should have grace toward our children—goodwill, benevolence, and a willingness to provide for all needs. But the writer of Hebrews tells us to come to the throne of grace to obtain grace to help in time of need (Hebrews 4:16). Only our Creator and Savior can dispense supernatural grace to his children. It is a parent's duty to be in the chain of command that encourages a child's access to the grace of God.

The first source of grace for a child is to have believing parents that are themselves living in the grace of God. Paul speaks of the need for a mother to not divorce her unbelieving husband, for if the children end up in a home under an unbeliever they are no longer sanctified as they were under a believing parent (1 Corinthians 7:13-15). To be sanctified is to be set apart by God for a special purpose. It is the state of being under a special dispensation of grace wherein God takes responsibility for the children. It is better for a person to live in misery with an unbelieving spouse than to remove one's children from the sanctification of grace that is guaranteed to a believer's children.

Nathan the Prophet

Kids can be very strange, each one unique. When our second son Nathan was just four years old, periodically he would wander around in the edge of the woods weeping and praying out loud. It got to be so commonplace that the other kids paid no attention to him when "the spirit moved him." He continued on and off until he was about seven or eight. It seems like a much bigger deal today as I write about it, but back then we just took it to be one of the normal peculiarities of a kid. Some play cowboy and Indians. Others play soldier. Nathan played prophet—quite sincerely. We didn't talk to him about it, or draw attention to it. We never mentioned it outside the home, and I don't remember us talking about it among ourselves other than maybe a bit of amusement when someone would ask where Nathan is and another kid would answer matter-of-factly, "Oh, he is walking around the pond praying." It was in a tone of like, "Well, you know how Nathan is." Now as a grown man in his thirties, it is Nathan who organizes the church to pray. It is he who speaks of the power of prayer. At four years of age Nathan had the grace of God upon him.

I hesitated to use this illustration because it is so far out of the mainstream. I do not want you to feel inadequate because you do not have a four-year-old prophet interceding for a lost and dying world. None of my other children were like Nathan in that regard and we did not feel they were any less spiritual. You may remember the story in *To Train Up A Child* about Nathan being a big liar when he was small. He was not a perfect child. He got plenty of spankings and was lazier than his older brother Gabriel, but he had the grace of God upon him in a unique manner.

Cross Current

There are times when having the grace of God upon you can save your life. When Rebekah was in New Guinea, Nathan returned for a visit to assist her for a couple months. While there, they took a trip down to the ocean and found a beautiful spot with a small white beach between some large rugged rocks. There were a few people around, but no one was swimming, so they jumped in. Everything went great until a cross current caught Nathan and swept him past the beach down in front of the wall of rocks. Large waves lifted him up and slammed him into the rocks. Rebekah stood helpless as she watched her little brother being tossed around in a merciless death trap. But on that day as on other days, the grace of God was upon him. When the waves tossed him up again, he was able to secure a hold on the rock face. He climbed higher so as to maintain his grip as the waves lifted up to dislodge him. He could not climb higher, so he held on while he got his breath and studied the waves. At the right moment he jumped back into the water and was carried away from the rock face where he swam parallel to the rocks and back to the beach area. He was beat up, but a whole lot wiser. The lesson he learned that day was that if the locals don't go there neither should you. Brother and sister gave God thanks.

The Road of Grace

When Rebekah was young we were still involved in an intensive ministry to the military. She recently mentioned to me something I had forgotten. Night after night, I would go out to the side of the road close to the Navy base in Millington, Tennessee and pray for the guys one by one as they walked past. They didn't know what I was doing. My head was not bowed. I was silent. Rebekah, five years old, sometimes sat beside me and prayed as well. There came a time when God moved me to begin witnessing to them. I created a sign that said "Ask me about Jesus" and nailed it to a telephone pole behind me. I put two folding chairs in front of me and sat there with Rebekah, still praying and waiting for someone to stop. Several guys would walk by, look at me with amusement, and one of them would say something like,

"Well, that's a different approach; I'll bite," and down he would sit. I had visual aids drawn that enabled me to explain the gospel in just five minutes. Over the summer, several guys got saved. We needed a place to meet with them and have Bible studies, so we rented an old nightclub just down the road from the base and opened it for nightly Bible studies. Hundreds of men were born again over the next eight or nine years. Just this week, I received an email from a man who introduced himself as one who was saved under that ministry and he wanted to thank me and re-establish contact.

First Rebekah and then the other children all joined us from time to time as we sat around tables and told the men about Jesus. My children often preached the gospel to guys fresh from boot camp, most of them just two months from the Bronx or L.A., or towns and cities and farms all over America, all headed to Vietnam. The kids sat in meetings where men testified with tears of their joy in finding Christ. Marines and Navy SEALs came to our house and swam in the pond with the kids. They played ball with us and ate at our dinner table. The kids lived in the midst of a stream of the flowing grace of God.

The grown children now laugh when they read accusations that homeschooled kids, ours in particular, are not properly socialized. Deb and I speak with a deep Southern accent, but none of the kids do. I have heard several people express curiosity, not being able to identify the accent of our children. It is a combination of 50 states and several foreign countries to which they were exposed growing up in our "cloistered" home.

Just as exposure to the Word of God will make a child wise, it will also place him in the stream of the grace of God. When children see terribly broken lives mended by the grace of God, they come to love God and value his grace above all. The Bible stories will be a constant stream of God's grace. The memorization of Scripture is vital to walking in grace. Faith that God cares and answers prayer is a door to more grace.

Gracie Full of Grace

Shalom's daughter Gracie has learned to access the grace of God like few children do. Shalom has taught her to ask God and expect an answer. At six years of age she has developed a reputation as an effectual prayer warrior. When she was just three, the family was traveling across Arkansas, headed back to middle Tennessee, when the van suddenly developed a loud knock symptomatic of a bent rod. For those not in the know, that means major engine failure, requiring a complete overhaul. Justin pulled over to the side of the interstate and turned off the noisy engine. Being a mechanic, he knew what it was and told the family that they were stranded. It was in the middle of night and a long way from home. As Justin got out of the van, Shalom turned to her three-year-old daughter and said, "Let's pray." They did. After not seeing any oil leaking onto the ground, Justin got back in and turned the ignition. The car started and ran without any knocking at all. It was amazing to a mechanic to have that kind of knock just disappear.

When they stopped at the next gas station there was a man standing there with a dirty white shirt with a large Bible reference printed on the back: Luke 18:27. Shalom pulled out her Bible and read the passage to Gracie, "The things which are impossible with men are possible with God." The van made it home in a few hours and Justin put it in the shop and found that a rod was indeed badly bent. The grace of God was upon them that night. Gracie's faith was built in that experience and in others that followed, so she began to pray, developing a history of answered prayer.

Federal Government Obeys God

In April 2011 Rick Batson, our missionary to the Philippines, was back in the states trying to renew his passport so he could get back to his ministry. Due to his past criminal record, he was having difficulty and had been delayed nearly three months. So he went to six-year-old Gracie and asked her to ask God to cause the government to get his passport to him. She prayed and asked God to get it there by Friday. Oops, kids don't know that it takes more than three days for a passport to be shipped from the east coast, not counting the time it takes to be processed. Friday, the mailman delivered one of those overnight packages containing his passport. It showed that Rick had paid for the overnight shipping, which he hadn't. We were all shocked at the answer to Gracie's prayer. None of us adults were naive enough to give God so little time to get the job done. But Gracie, full of grace, had expected a Friday delivery. "A little child shall lead them."

Dog Food Delivery

Recently, Gracie said to her mother, "We need some dog food." Shalom responded, "Yeah, and I need some herbs from Aunt Shoshanna's store.

Daddy is in town and I had mentioned that I needed the herbs." Well, Gracie-full-of-grace said, "Let's pray and ask God to tell Daddy to get some dog food and herbs." They prayed. When Justin arrived home they asked where the herbs and dog food were. He made an exasperated gesture indicating that he knew he was forgetting something and said, "I pulled into the herb store knowing there was something I needed to get, but I couldn't remember what it was."

Hands on her hips Gracie asked, "Well, what about the dog food?"

Gracie's poor Daddy looked pained, "Oh, I remembered I was supposed to get it, but someone stopped to talk, causing me to forget."

That is not right; God is supposed to answer prayer. A little later young Gracie walked up to the office and Talitha said, "I just came from town and remembered that you were out of dog food, so I bought some for you."

Gracie went back home and told her mother and then added, "Well, I guess Talitha listens to God better than Daddy."

The church has a prayer meeting every Tuesday night, and Gracie goes to pray with the adults. Her parents have put her in a path wherein she is growing in wisdom and the grace of God is upon her. What more could you ask? What greater blessing is there?

Songs of Grace

Another way to put your children in the fountain of grace is through Holy Spirit inspired music. The church has entered a post-spiritual era in regard to music. It is addicted to mediocrity and carnality in music.

Give me two paragraphs to sound off, and then I will get back to the subject. When I was young and kids from the church got together, we all gathered around a piano or guitar and sang for hours. The old hymns and choruses lifted our hearts and spirits to God. Back then, music was something ordinary people did together. It was not a spectator sport, not a staged event for entertainment. It was group-centered and everyone could participate. In recent years, several young people in our church have learned to play the guitar and none of them can lead us in singing. Their music is not people friendly. God would say, "Who's making that noise?"

Over the last forty years the church has adopted the nightclub concept. Singers don't want to lead others in songs of worship and praise; they want to perform like Elvis or the Beatles. The singing, swaying congregation is just staging for their performance. Churches are now set up like nightclubs and "worship leaders" are "stars" performing. Since the early seventies, not much has been written or performed that fills us with the grace of God. New music that does not come out of a revival most likely originates from a love of music rather than a love of God.

I go to the prisons and minister. The Sunday services have an entirely different crowd than the Bible studies I conduct on Saturday. Many of the believers will not attend the Sunday service, because they do not like to stand beside a Sodomite or a gang leader who is rocking and swaying to the music, clapping his hands and saying "Hallelujah". The typical worship music as sung in most churches appeals to every sort in the prison, without prejudice.

I have stood before a group of drunks and dopeheads as we sang Amazing Grace or Power in the Blood and watched them weep in conviction, many coming to Christ, but I have never seen anyone come under conviction listening to the repetitive modern church music.

When I tune the radio to a "Christian music" channel, I find most of the songs offensive and fleshly and would rather listen to country, folk, bluegrass, or classic. Actually, I listen to nothing.

But there are still plenty of good old hymns and spiritual songs available on the web for download. Fill your home with music God would appreciate and you will shower your children with grace. Mothers, sing with your kids. Sponsor kids' meetings where there is lots of old fashioned camp style singing. The Spirit of God in me loves the joyful marching beat and four-part harmony of the great hymns and spiritual songs.

"Let the word of Christ dwell in you richly in all wisdom; teaching and admonishing one another in psalms and hymns and spiritual songs, singing with grace in your hearts to the Lord" (Colossians 3:16).

There it is, "singing with grace in your hearts to the Lord." What is the right music? It is the music that puts grace in hearts unto the Lord. When music fills you with Jesus it is Holy Spirit inspired.

One day not long ago I was out in the yard when I heard a song in the air. I stopped to listen. It was Gracie in her yard about a hundred yards away. "Trust and obey, for there's no other way to be happy in Jesus, but to trust and obey. What a fellowship sweet, as we sit at his feet..." I picked up the song and sung with her. I heard her voice rise and we sang a duet with a thousand angels between us listening and God in heaven receiving back the grace he had given.

Fellowship of Grace

Another fantastic source of grace is the sweet fellowship of believers. I am at home with believers whose minds are on the Lord, who are ready to express their gratitude for his mercies and ready to share a word of testimony of what God is doing. Children raised in an atmosphere of praise will never grow up to be bitter and resentful. "Looking diligently lest any man fail of the grace of God; lest any root of bitterness springing up trouble you, and thereby many be defiled" (Hebrews 12:15).

As we abide in fellowship one with the other, we increase the light and create a cleansing atmosphere for our children. "But if we walk in the light, as he is in the light, we have fellowship one with another, and the blood of Jesus Christ his Son cleanseth us from all sin" (1 John 1:7–8).

The joy and love of the brethren is a rain shower of grace on children that gives them the strength to face the difficulties of life. "Thou therefore, my son, be strong in the grace that is in Christ Jesus" (2 Timothy 2:1).

Our words carry grace or grumbling, complaining or exclaiming his virtues. "Let your speech be alway with grace, seasoned with salt" (Colosians 4:6). Our children will partake of our grace (Philippians 1:7; Ephesians 4:29).

You, parent, are the one who runs the spiritual bath water for your children. You either bathe them in the love and grace of God, or you bathe them in the darkness of your own soul. How will they ever be filled with grace if you, sir, are filled with pornography or other secret sins? Repent and come to the well and draw water of joy and abundance.

Not all adults are the same. In the last days some will arise from the grave to shame and everlasting contempt and some to life everlasting (Daniel 12:2).

Every child is somebody's baby, somebody's little boy or girl. They were all cultured by their parents and are a product of their upbringing. Are your children filled with the grace of God? If not, why not? What will you do today that will make a difference now and in eternity? Order my audio messages "Righteousness," or listen to my Romans messages online free of charge.

THE FIFTH PILLAR:

In Favor With God

In Favor With God

After Jesus' visit to the temple at 12 years of age, we read:

"And Jesus increased in wisdom and stature, and in favour with God and man" (Luke 2:52). The child Jesus increased in favor with God.

The Son of God is not the only one who found favor with God. For we read, "And the child Samuel grew on, and was in favour both with the LORD, and also with men" (1 Samuel 2:26). God's favor toward Samuel started when he was yet just a small boy. Remember God speaking to the boy Samuel while he slept. God's favor was seen in the way God supported his prophetic ministry. "And Samuel grew, and the LORD was with him, and did let none of his words fall to the ground" (1 Samuel 3:19).

God favored Noah, as seen in the fact that he "found grace in the eyes of the Lord" (Genesis 6:8) and was given instruction on how to survive the coming destruction.

I. Highly Favored

Abraham, Highly Favored

Abraham was a man highly favored of God, and he made reference to that favor and used it as leverage to get God and two angels to stay for supper: "And said, My Lord, if now I have found favour in thy sight, pass not away, I pray thee, from thy servant" (Genesis 18:3). Those same divine visitors expressed God's favor toward Abraham by including him in the circle of those who knew of the coming destruction on Sodom (Genesis 18:19).

God stated the reason Abraham was favored: "For I know him, that he will command his children and his household after him, and they shall keep the way of the LORD, to do justice and judgment; that the LORD may bring upon Abraham that which he hath spoken of him" (Genesis 18:19). God was partial to Abraham because he was a good child trainer and would impart his faith to his children.

God even favored Abraham after he had foolishly placed his wife Sarah in jeopardy by deceiving king Abimelech about his relationship to her. It is amazing that God's favor did not diminish even when Abraham was a disobedient liar (Genesis 20). God still supported him.

Later God favored Abraham with a child in his old age (Genesis 21:2). Then God favored Abraham's seed, not only Isaac but Ishmael as well.

God favored Abraham with a term of endearment reserved for no other, calling him "the Friend of God". "And the Scripture was fulfilled which saith, Abraham believed God, and it was imputed unto him for righteousness: and he was called the Friend of God" (James 2:23). See also 2 Chronicles 20:7.

135

Favor Passed on to the Next Generation

God favors the children of those whom he favors. "And the LORD appeared unto him the same night, and said, I am the God of Abraham thy father: fear not, for I am with thee, and will bless thee, and multiply thy seed for my servant Abraham's sake" (Genesis 26:24).

Because of Abraham's faith, God favored his grandson Jacob in the multiplication of his herds, and then granted him favor with his angry brother whom he had deceived.

Parent, if you obey God and live by faith, committing yourself, your resources, and your children to God, when the time comes God will favor them for your sake.

God granted Israel, Abraham's descendents, favor with the Egyptians. "And I will give this people favour in the sight of the Egyptians: and it shall come to pass, that, when ye go, ye shall not go empty: But every woman shall borrow of her neighbour, and of her that sojourneth in her house, jewels of silver, and jewels of gold, and raiment: and ye shall put them upon your sons, and upon your daughters; and ye shall spoil the Egyptians" (Exodus 3:21–22).

To this day the descendents of Abraham, Isaac, and Jacob are "beloved for the fathers' sakes" (Romans 11:28). Remember, God favored Abraham, because he knew Abraham would teach his children after him (Genesis 18:19).

Blessed Coming and Going

God blessed my father in his life and in his death. That blessing passed on to his children, and to his children's children. My father was not a perfect man, but he was

136

a blessed man. Likewise, neither my children nor I are perfect, but we are blessed, highly favored of God.

When Deb and I were married, a good friend taking part in the wedding read and expounded upon a passage that has become our life's theme.

Deuteronomy 28:2–7:

2 And all these blessings shall come on thee, and overtake thee, if thou shalt hearken unto the voice of the LORD thy God.

3 Blessed shalt thou be in the city, and blessed shalt thou be in the field.

4 Blessed shall be the fruit of thy body, and the fruit of thy ground, and the fruit of thy cattle, the increase of thy kine, and the flocks of thy sheep.

5 Blessed shall be thy basket and thy store.

6 Blessed shalt thou be when thou comest in, and blessed shalt thou be when thou goest out.

7 The LORD shall cause thine enemies that rise up against thee to be smitten before thy face: they shall come out against thee one way, and flee before thee seven ways.

I love this passage. I can feel the favor of God by just reading it. When I rise up and lie down, when I come in and go out, when I am in the city or in the field, it makes no difference, the blessings of God are upon me.

I am going to reveal a little secret. I have felt my entire life was one of extreme blessing. I have felt that I am a reverse Job experiment. As if, when I was a child, Satan came before the Lord, and God said, "Have you considered my little child Mike?"

And the Devil said, "Yes, but if you bless him and he does not suffer or experience any losses, he will forget you. If you bless him and his children, he will take you for granted and get a big head, blown up with pride. If you bless him financially he will become avaricious. If you bless him with gifts he will use them for his glory and forget the eternal. I dare you to bless him. He can't take it."

Like Job there have been times when I have had to fall on my face and repent in dust and ashes, and like Job there have been times God has had to rebuke me, but I count that as part of the blessing, "For whom the Lord loveth he chasteneth, and scourgeth every son whom he receiveth" (Hebrews 12:6). I count myself all the more blessed when God chastens me, for he deals with me as with a son. The beautiful thing about it is not that I am blessed, but that I see blessings on my children and their children, seeming to grow stronger with each generation.

My story is not at all unique. I could walk you through the church on Sunday morning and introduce you to family after family that is equally blessed. They have planted seed in their children and are bearing beautiful fruit. I have met many families from all over the world that are equally blessed of God, highly favored. It is the nature of God to favor his own, those whom he has purchased with his blood (Romans 8:32). The river of blessing is big enough to accommodate all. "Therefore with joy shall ye draw water out of the wells of salvation" (Isaiah 12:3).

Pass On the Blessing

You can pass on the blessings by blessing. Bless God with your whole heart. Your children should hear your praise and thanksgiving. You don't need to make a show of it. But when you feel the blessings of God, say so. Ask for his blessings in prayer. Stand publicly in church and bless God. In the course of the day, without being religious, just make mention of God's goodness in the presence of your children. "I will go in the strength of the Lord GOD: I will make mention of thy righteousness, even of thine only." (Psalm 71:16).

If your children are going to find favor with God, you must provide God with a reason. Why should he favor your children? Not because of your personal interest. God favors those who favor what he favors. God favors love, joy, peace, righteousness, judgment, mercy, grace, and obedience. Access God's blessings and you become a conduit for the blessings on your children. There is no other way.

Just yesterday, Deb walked into Shalom's house and observed Justin as he leaned over the desk, staring at the computer, frozen in complete concentration as he studied a cut-away drawing of all the parts of an engine. Twenty-month-old Parker sat in his lap staring at the screen, equally absorbed in concentration. Occasionally Parker would screw his head around to look into his daddy's face and then return his attention to the screen. The boy had no idea what he was looking at, but he was content to be sharing the experience with his daddy. There is not a better time to impart your values and interests to your children than between the ages of eighteen months and five years.

When eight-year-old Gabriel left his outside fun and walked into the house in the middle of the day to tell his mother that he "wanted to learn to read the Bible like Daddy," he was choosing to improve his access to God. "The LORD taketh pleasure in them that fear him, in those that hope in his mercy" (Psalm 147:11).

Highly Favored in Marriage

About seventeen years ago, Deb and I were invited to Fort Worth, Texas to teach the book of Romans in a small church. A thirteen-year-old boy came up to us and said he wanted to learn to witness, so we gathered all the young people together and took them to the local mall where we gave out tracts and preached the gospel. The management ran us off, but not before we distributed about a thousand tracts. Years later, Joshua pointed to that experience as the beginning of his ministry. About three years later, on another visit to the church, we went with Joshua as he preached in a very large homeless shelter. In time, he went to the mission field in Ukraine and has been there since March 2001. I have had occasion to observe many young men, and I know of no one who has been more singularly minded and committed than this young man, Joshua Steele. He was the most morally earnest and circumspect young man I have known.

After getting his ministry well established, he felt it was time to find favor of God in taking a wife. Don't tell me you didn't know that you gain God's favor by taking a wife…"Whoso findeth a wife findeth a good thing, and obtaineth favour of the LORD" (Proverbs 18:22). So he notified his parents that he was ready to get married. Meanwhile, there was a beautiful, intelligent, talented treasure who loved the Lord and wanted to be a missionary, also of the age of marriage. With Joshua faithfully laboring in Ukraine, God brought the two families together and with prayer and common sense, they decided it was a match. Joshua was called home to meet his prospective bride, and from the start it was truly a marriage made in heaven.

I have seen some of these "arranged" marriages and most of them had everything arranged but the happiness of the loveless couple, but this was one of those unique times that God favored both.

When I arrived for the wedding dinner, my eyes nearly popped out. She was beautiful and as bright as the sunshine. They loved each other and hit it off from the start. There was no kissing or hugging until after the "I dos," but they have been hot ever since, now trailing three children. They are in Ukraine as I write, with an ever-expanding ministry. I have continued to support Joshua and recognize that he is a man highly favored of God.

Just a thought to all of your "wanna-get-marrieds" out there: God does not give one of his highly favored to one who is not so highly favored. God does not equally favor all. "The steps of a good man are ordered by the LORD: and he delighteth in his way" (Psalm 37:23). "Delight thyself also in the LORD; and he shall give thee the desires of thine heart." (There are conditions you must meet to be highly favored of God.) "Commit thy way unto the LORD; trust also in him; and he shall bring it to pass" (Psalm 37:4–5).

Daniel, a Man Greatly Beloved

Daniel was carried into a foreign country to be a slave. While in confinement, God granted young Daniel favor with his masters.

"Now God had brought Daniel into favour and tender love with the prince of the eunuchs. And the prince of the eunuchs said unto Daniel, I fear my lord the king, who hath appointed your meat and your drink: for why should he see your faces worse liking than the children which are of your sort? then shall ye make me endanger my head to the king" (Daniel 1:9–10).

Daniel was staunchly faithful to the law of God and everyone was aware of it. Three different times the holy angels told Daniel that he is "greatly beloved"—a very special status that garnered the attention of the angels in a unique way.

Daniel's favor with God resulted in answered prayer.

"At the beginning of thy supplications the commandment came forth, and I am come to shew thee; for thou art greatly beloved: therefore understand the matter, and consider the vision" (Daniel 9:23).

Daniel's favor with God resulted in God giving him supernatural understanding.

"And he said unto me, O Daniel, a man greatly beloved, understand the words that I speak unto thee, and stand upright: for unto thee am I now sent" (Daniel 10:11).

Daniel's favor with God resulted in his receiving strength of spirit from heaven.

"And said, O man greatly beloved, fear not: peace be unto thee, be strong, yea, be strong. And when he had spoken unto me, I was strengthened, and said, Let my lord speak; for thou hast strengthened me" (Daniel 10:19).

Answered prayer, understanding, and personal inner strength are three wonderful gifts from God reserved for one who was greatly beloved and highly favored.

Job

When Satan came before God to challenge his credibility with the human race, God bragged on the faithfulness and righteousness of his servant Job. Accepting a challenge from Satan, God allowed the Accuser to inflict Job with unspeakable suffering and loss. Three of his friends continually urged him to recognize that his suffering was due to his sins—which it wasn't. But through it all, Job was faithful, saying, "Thou hast granted me life and favour, and thy visitation hath preserved my spirit" (Job 10:12).

After a great length of time, God vindicated Job by saying to his accusers, "and my servant Job shall pray for you: for him will I accept: lest I deal with you after your folly, in that ye have not spoken of me the thing which is right, like my servant Job" (Job 42:8).

God favored Job in his patient faith and restored him to wealth, giving him another family. "Behold, we count them happy which endure. Ye have heard of the patience of Job, and have seen the end of the Lord; that the Lord is very pitiful, and of tender mercy" (James 5:11). "For his anger endureth but a moment; in his favour is life: weeping may endure for a night, but joy cometh in the morning" (Psalm 30:5).

Old Enough?

Jesus said, "Suffer the little children to come unto me, and forbid them not: for of such is the kingdom of God. Verily I say unto you, Whosoever shall not receive the kingdom of God as a little child, he shall not enter therein" (Mark 10:14–15). Take note: Jesus commanded us to bring the little children to him, telling us they are able to receive the Kingdom of God. While parents are waiting for their children to "get old enough" to know God, they are becoming thoroughly acquainted with the world.

I look at some two-year-olds and I see the light of God. I look at others and see the shadows of darkness covering their souls. Parents call them brats; the devil calls them his own. Jesus invites them to come, but parents think they are not old enough. It is a great pity to be a parent and not train up your children to be in favor with God. Parents are entirely responsible for their child's development and training.

"The LORD taketh pleasure in them that fear him, in those that hope in his mercy" (Psalm 147:11). And that includes children. When a five-year-old is embarrassed to talk about God or to pray, that little soul is not neutral. It is already on the side of darkness and "will not come to the light, because his deeds are evil" (John 3:19-21). For "The light of the righteous rejoiceth…" (Proverbs 13:9).

It is easy to pass religious dogma to your children. That can be done by having them memorize a catechism, and by consistent indoctrination into a given religion. But it is not indoctrination into religion that we advocate. Children can have the spirit of God and know him as well as can an adult.

Satisfied Children

Some people boast of being in a position to receive political or judicial favors, but to know your child being favored by God has no equal. The greatest security a child can have is for God to favor him. "For in his favour is life" (Psalm 30:5). Job said, "Thou hast granted me life and favour, and thy visitation hath preserved my spirit" (Job 10:12). God preserves those whom he favors and he grants them "life more abundantly."

Deep satisfaction is to be found living in God's favor, for Moses said Naphtali was "satisfied with favour, and full with the blessing of the LORD" (Deuteronomy 33:23). Children living in God's favor are never discontent and angry. They are satisfied. The beauty and joy of having satisfied children is an unspeakable pleasure to parents.

Deb and I have five children. All five are very happily married and have produced 19 grandkids so far. All of the grandkids seem to be well satisfied with their parents' favor and with God's blessings. "For the LORD taketh pleasure in his people..." (Psalm 149:4).

Motivating God to Favor Us

God takes pleasure in those that take pleasure in him. God told us why he took pleasure in David: "...the LORD hath sought him a man after his own heart..." (1 Samuel 13:14). "I entreated thy favour with my whole heart: be merciful unto me according to thy word" (Psalm 119:58). David valued what God values. He wanted to be in the center of God's will. He tells us, "For the LORD loveth judgment, and forsaketh not his saints; they are preserved for ever: but the seed of the wicked shall be cut off" (Psalm 37:28). God favored David, because he knew that "The LORD taketh pleasure in them that fear him, in those that hope in his mercy" (Psalm 147:11). "The steps of a good man are ordered by the LORD: and he delighteth in his way" (Psalm 37:23). David delighted in God and God delighted in David, showing him favor.

God's favor even provided for David's chastisement when he sinned.

"For whom the LORD loveth he correcteth; even as a father the son in whom he delighteth" (Proverbs 3:12).

Pleasing God with Righteousness

Between public schools and television, most of this present generation of young people is unmoored and completely lost. But there is still a remnant of young people being raised up to love God and all that is holy and pure.

"For the righteous LORD loveth righteousness; his countenance doth behold the upright" (Psalm 11:7). It is not an easy battle, but God loves champions of righteousness, kids who will fight sin in their own lives like David fought Goliath. The "LORD loveth the righteous" (Psalm 146:8) and will support them with the full power of heaven. If you want your children to find favor with God, raise them up to be righteous.

THE SIXTH PILLAR:

In Favor With Men

Favor With Men

We have been examining this amazing Biblical outline for rearing our children.

We read, "And Jesus increased in wisdom and stature, and in favour with God and man" (Luke 2:52). If we train our children in accordance with the five concepts we have discussed it will result in them finding favor with man.

I hear someone challenging, "Why should I care about finding favor with men? All I care about is favor with God." That's fine unless you plan on living in this world before you go to heaven. In that case, having the favor of your fellow man can certainly make life easier and more productive. We are living in an alien world, but we are here as ambassadors of Christ. We represent him and as such, we desire to present a favorable view of his kingdom. We would be poor ambassadors indeed if everyone disliked us and stood against our endeavors.

The Bible abounds with examples of his servants garnering extra favor with the people and those in power. Of the early church we read, "And they, continuing daily with one accord in the temple, and breaking bread from house to house, did eat their meat with gladness and singleness of heart, Praising God, and having favour with all the people. And the Lord added to the church daily such as should be saved" (Acts 2:46–47). The founding church was presenting a new concept to the Jews, and they needed the favor of the people.

King Solomon wrote, "When a man's ways please the LORD, he maketh even his enemies to be at peace with him" (Proverbs 16:7). Due to our stand for righteousness and truth, we will have enemies. There will be those who are jealous. Some will resent our popularity. Others will be envious of our success. Some men just despise the truth and are antagonized by our lack of compromise on issues. But many Biblical examples demonstrate that even our avowed enemies will be soothed to peace when our ways please the Lord.

I. Peacemaker

Joseph the Peacemaker

Genesis 39:20–23:

20 And Joseph's master took him, and put him into the prison, a place where the king's prisoners were bound: and he was there in the prison.

21 But the LORD was with Joseph, and shewed him mercy, and gave him favour in the sight of the keeper of the prison.

22 And the keeper of the prison committed to Joseph's hand all the prisoners that were in the prison; and whatsoever they did there, he was the doer of it.

23 The keeper of the prison looked not to any thing that was under his hand; because the LORD was with him, and that which he did, the LORD made it to prosper.

Joseph was a slave in a strange land. He had enemies who falsely accused him and threw him into prison. His ways so pleased the Lord that he found favor with God and men. He demonstrated such integrity and wisdom that he gained the complete trust of the prison authorities. They made him the chief warden, and he handled the day-to-day operation of the prison. Joseph had found favor in the sight of his captors.

In time Joseph garnered favor from Pharaoh himself, being exalted to a place in the kingdom directly under the king. Joseph had caused his enemies to be at peace with him, finding favor with men.

Joseph was a hard worker, he was wise in his decision making and he obviously treated people with respect. People have a natural pleasure in a man of this quality.

Daniel

Daniel was another young man that was dragged away from his home to be a slave in a foreign land. He soon demonstrated such wisdom and understanding that he found favor in the eyes of his master, being exalted to a place of prominence as a trusted advisor to the king.

When other advisors to the king grew jealous of Daniel's acclaim, they manipulated the law to place Daniel in jeopardy for praying to his God. Reluctantly the Persian king had to honor the law and throw Daniel in the lions' den, but only after he spent many hours searching the law books, hoping to find a legal loophole that would permit him to release Daniel. The king so cared for Daniel that he appeared at the entrance of the lions' den first thing in the morning after spending the night fasting (Daniel 6:18-19). Finding Daniel well and praising his God, the king released him and had his enemies thrown in the den, where they were promptly eaten. Daniel had favor with God and with the king.

The Principle of Favor With Men

Jesus related the principle whereby one can find favor with men.

"Give, and it shall be given unto you; good measure, pressed down, and shaken together, and running over, shall men give into your bosom. For with the same measure that ye mete withal it shall be measured to you again" (Luke 6:38).

"Give, and it shall be given." The imagery is taken from the marketplace where men are buying and selling. When you sell a product, give a good measure. Make sure the basket used to measure is pressed down to compact it, shaken together so as to further settle the contents, increasing the amount in the basket, and then running over. If you sell in that liberal manner men will sell back to you with equal generosity. If you are stingy, they will be stingy. I can tell you from experience, you can make a half bushel of peas fill up a bushel basket by fluffing the contents, or you can get a bushel and a half in a basket by pressing it down, shaking it together, and allowing it to run over. Men take note of your stinginess or liberality and will return it to you in increased measure. If you are stingy, men will be stingier. If you are liberal, they will be more liberal.

In our country community I know tightfisted, stingy people who stay poor and are not looked upon with favor by their neighbors. No one will go out of their way to assist them. Then I know others who will give you the first ripe tomato from their vines, and everybody relates to them by adding an extra measure. The man who protects his store stays poor, whereas the man who gives freely will never be needy.

How do we teach our children to be givers and not takers? It's simple; the principle Jesus related is applicable in the home as well as the marketplace. When your children see you sacrificing for them, they will sacrifice for you and for their brothers and sisters. The home that has a habit of tending to the needs of others produces children who find it "more blessed to give than to receive" and will therefore find favor with men.

It is not wise to run your home like the Socialists run the country. Do not constrain your children to give. Do not shame them for choosing not to give. When citizens of the state are forced to part with their money so it can be indiscriminately given to those who have less, the people resent it for the same reasons you would resent having your first ripe tomato taken from you by force and given to a lazy bum who does not plant a garden and smokes three packs a day. Giving is like love; it cannot be dictated or demanded. It is granted freely from the heart or it doesn't exist.

You must cultivate the heart of your child through example and Bible teaching. Example is important, not only in the home but also in their social life. If children are raised with friends who are stingy and self-indulging, they will develop a worldview of "do to them before they do to you."

Green Bananas and Jungle Manners

I will never forget an experience I had when living in the jungles of Belize for two months with two other fellows. We were back in the bush, living in a very primitive Maya Indian village, erecting a building in preparation for the coming of a medical missionary. We had plenty of canned food available but no meat except what we killed, which was not much, and no fresh vegetables or fruit. It was 100 degrees or more every day and humid beyond belief. We were covered with bug bites, bored, overworked, and miserable.

Then a missionary stopped by and gave us a whole stalk of green bananas. We tried one right away but they were too bitter to eat. So we hung the stalk up as instructed and waited for them to ripen. You cannot imagine how much that stalk of bananas meant to us. It was like we had been lost and were now saved. In a couple days a banana began to show just a little yellow. Every hour we watched it turn. Several others began to turn yellow. Oh, but we were excited, just a couple more days and

we would have ripe bananas. In the afternoon I came back from the river and found the one partially-ripened banana gone. One of the guys had eaten the green banana. The next morning two or three of the other bananas that were beginning to turn were also gone. So I waited till noon and picked the one partially yellow banana. At home I would never have eaten such a green piece of fruit, and it was not very good, but it was much better than nothing, so I ate the hard green thing, feeling some satisfaction that I was keeping them from getting it. Within a few days we had eaten the entire stalk of green bananas, experienced significant bowel purges, and never tasted a ripe banana.

What is interesting is that though the stalk was hanging up right in the middle of the camp none of us ever saw the other picking and eating a banana. It was all done on the sly. I laugh at us now, but at the time I was seriously upset with the two selfish guys that made me eat green bananas on the sneak. Neither of those guys had my favor nor I theirs. When I see them today, thirty years later, I wonder if they are eating green bananas before their kids get a chance. They probably wonder the same of me.

The Ornery Boy

Some time ago there was a family that attended our church and they had a very selfish son about four years old. I will call him Jehu, since I don't know anyone named Jehu who would be offended. He was the best example of a kid not having favor with men. At the time Deb and I discussed it, trying to figure out what his parents did to make him so ornery, but we just didn't know the family well enough to come to any informed conclusions. It still stumps us to this day.

Jehu would go to another kid's birthday party and try to open the gifts. When he saw something that struck his fancy he would grab it and not let go until constrained by force. His shenanigans provided significant distractions in the church meetings. Our meetings were informal, with family groups sitting around in various chairs or couches facing to the center. Every family that had children tried to sit some distance from Jehu, for he always tried to take things away from the other kids.

Jehu was never satisfied with his own stuff. He wanted anything that was of interest to another child. He had snatched so many objects from the other kids that they watched him like a chicken watches the sky for hawks. They would turn their backs to him and hold their coloring books or dolls close to them so he could not swoop down and snatch them away. And that is exactly what he would do. The moment a child became distracted and laid his possession down, Jehu would slyly move close and sweep it away, grinning with satisfaction. Then he would retreat back to his lair at his parent's feet and fiddle with the object while he observed the owner's consternation. If the deprived child showed no emotion about losing the object, Jehu quickly lost interest, relinquishing the toy, and transferred his focus to another kid's possession where he would repeat his banditry.

In Favor With Men

Deb observed an interesting exchange one Sunday. He had snatched a toy from a four-year-old girl and sat some distance away enjoying her pain. In our church there was a five-year-old girl, very mature for her age, who conducted herself with great pause and self-control, and who had been the victim of the bandit before and had learned to be on guard. She saw that the little four-year-old girl was deeply hurt by Jehu's dashing thievery. So, while Deb observed, the five-year-old heroine picked up an object that held no interest to her and began to play with it like it was much fun. When she saw Jehu lusting after it and starting to move her way, she extended it toward him. As he reached out his left hand to receive it she quietly took the little girl's toy from his other hand. He didn't even notice that he had given it up. The bigger girl handled the exchange like a professional spy. It was as smooth as silk. As she turned away she was grinning ever so subtly, enjoying her non-confrontational victory. She got up and walked a few steps, handing the toy back to the victim of his theft and then glided back to stand sentinel over her brother and his possessions. Deb was amazed and amused at the whole event. She could see adult character already formed in the kids involved. Jehu the Terrible and the girl diplomat had met on the battlefield, and the diplomat won without any bloodshed.

The thief sitting in his lair, caressing his new prize, looked up to discover that no one cared for his recent acquisition, so he dropped it and swept the room to see who had a coveted possession that could be pilfered. This is the behavior of a child that evolves into a thief, the kind that can afford what he needs, but just gets a thrill out of taking.

No one liked the kid, and most people transferred their dislike to the parents. In time we moved on and lost contact. That kid never had favor with men, or with women and small children. He grew up to be a bully, still without favor. I can't really tell you what caused that young boy to be so selfish, but he did grow up to lack self discipline and to become a thief. Everyone but his parents could see the boy had problems. Today they would tell you that they "raised their kids right." It is "just his sinful nature" that caused his deviant behavior.

The young diplomat had favor with everyone who observed the event that day and she maintained that favor as she grew into a lovely young lady.

Who Doesn't Like Kids?

I do indeed enjoy children, especially from about two to five years old. They are an endless source of entertainment. Their curiosity is captivating. I love to introduce them to the wonders of the world about them. But I also enjoy some of the boys as they grow older. I will admit, there are some kids I just do not like and do not want to spend any time with them. They do not have my favor. I am kind to all children and generous with them, but there are some kids that I will seek out, because they are interesting.

I do not feel guilty or inadequate for not favoring all children equally. Jesus had three special disciples, but only one of whom it is said "Jesus loved" (John 13:23). I assure you, it is completely normal and quite emotionally sound to favor some children over others. Just as we like and favor some adults and not others, so we like and favor some kids.

Answer these questions to yourself. Do you like your kids? Do other people like them? Do adults strike up a conversation with your children? Do you have one child that people like and one they don't favor as much? How are they different? What is likeable about the one and unlikeable about the other? Now what can you do to change the less-favored child?

Making Children Attractive

An attractive person is a well-favored person, and I am not talking about looks. Good looks provide an immediate attraction, but that attraction won't last if the child has an unattractive spirit.

Several things make a child attractive to me. The first is a strong spirit. I like spunk. I am drawn to a child that is bold and confident. I like to see a four-year-old speak up boldly and have an opinion. I am going to spend time talking to that kid.

Just this month a family came by to visit and a boy about five years old walked up to me and straightway asked, "Do you love Jesus?" He got my attention. "Yes, I love Jesus; thanks for asking." I took time to teach him how to throw knives.

A strong-spirited child is attractive to everyone. They have intestinal fortitude, otherwise known as guts. When I go to the creek with kids and they dive in with boldness, they instantly gain my favor. When a visiting kid says, "Can I help?" he's got me from the start. When a child plays a musical instrument or paints a picture or bakes a loaf of bread he, or she, has my favor. When I take a child on a ride in my Kubota four-wheeler and she whoops in joy, she has my favor. In other words, when a child is alive and enjoying life with no complaints they have my favor.

The short of it is, we all like interesting people. We like interesting children. Children are interesting when they are inquisitive and involved in life. A boring child that is unhappy is not favored by anyone.

Training Children to Be Strong in Spirit

Everyone enjoys someone who is ready to help work with an enthusiastic cheer. You just know that the child who says "May I help?" has a spark of wonder in his soul. Even in our place of business the laborer who enjoys his job and works extra because he loves seeing a thing finished, has favor with the other workers and with the boss. An adult with this kind of heart will be more likely to impart the same to his children.

Now, if a child really wants to gain my favor, ask me a Bible question or a question about God. If a kid loves the Lord and the Word of God, he has my full attention. When Gracie stands in the yard singing a hymn, she has my attention. When she prays expecting an answer, she has my complete attention.

The passage tells us that after Jesus' visit to the temple he increased in favor with man. He had just spent three days asking and answering questions when it tells us of his gaining favor with man. Can you imagine how this twelve-year-old boy asking thoughtful and relevant questions and then answering some that they posed captivated the learned men? He had their complete favor.

If you have a boring child that garners no favor, make him or her interesting. A child is favored who looks an adult in the eyes and makes a serious and relevant statement. Attend to the intellectual part of your children.

The best and most immediate road to making a child interesting is talking to her. Don't leave your daughters to grow up to be brainless cooks and sweepers. Your home should be full of ideas with plenty of discussion on issues of every sort. They should form opinions and learn to defend their views.

Broad experiences make a child interesting and gain favor. As of this writing Jeremiah is five years old. He will walk up to a complete stranger in a store and tell him what herbs to take to relieve his cough. People are shocked and amazed. Sometimes he gets it wrong or can't quite pronounce the name of the herb, appealing to his mother or father for assistance, but he is not the least bit embarrassed to offer unsolicited assistance to a total stranger.

I don't know where the old saying originated, "Children should be seen and not heard." Children should be seen, heard, hugged, laughed at, chased, told stories, taken by the hand, and led into a world of joy and wonder. Leave the adults to molt away and collect cobwebs, but "Suffer the little children to come unto me, and forbid them not: for of such is the kingdom of God" (Mark 10:14). "And the streets of the city shall be full of boys and girls playing in the streets thereof" (Zechariah 8:5).

A Good Name

"A good name is rather to be chosen than great riches, and loving favour rather than silver and gold" (Proverbs 22:1). A good name comes from a good life. It is accumulated through many years of faithfulness and integrity. But a bad name is earned by just one experience. I know a child who is reported to have acted in a sexually deviant manner. No one trusts him even though it is many years later. He does not have a good name and is not highly favored.

I know a young lady of marriageable age. When she was just going through puberty, I overheard her making scathing remarks to her sister. Her tone and manner was filled with venom and anger. I held her in good favor until that moment. After seeing her spirit thus displayed, I will never tell a young man seeking a wife that she would be good for him. She lost my recommendation through that one glimpse of her soul. I don't write her off as a person

161

or a friend. I would never deprive her of the normal affection and respect given to friends, but I just could not recommend her to a young man whom I value.

From time to time I hire young men to help me on the farm. Some are already skilled and able, while others are unskilled and inept. I am not put off by a kid who knows nothing and is not worth the price of his dinner, if he is willing to work. But no matter the skill level, if I find a fifteen-year-old boy who is lazy and does not have the integrity to give me an hour's effort for an hour's pay, he loses my favor. Several years later, when a young lady asks me if he would be a suitable husband, I will say, "Not unless you want to live on food stamps or bum off friends and relatives."

You must teach your children the importance of having a good name. It will carry them through a world of difficulty. Just as I shared stories and impressions here in this book, I likewise communicated with my children as they were growing up. When we heard about a boy looking at pornography, I would say, "Well, he has spoiled his soul; he will never marry one of my daughters." If a girl was caught lying, we discussed the evils of being deceptive and how she will always be known as a liar. If a boy was lazy, I spoke of him as something akin to a thief, "not worth his salt." My children were schooled in the need to maintain a good name. It was not just theory; it was real people around us who picked up labels and lost or gained favor with men.

Lazy Losers

Lazy people are never highly favored. Everybody respects hard work, except an unhappy wife who wants more attention. But that is for another book. I can't help it; I just love hard working kids. I don't expect them to endure the drudgery of endless work on the level of an adult, but I like to see a will to work. The five-year-old may not last but five minutes on a hard job, but that initial willingness earns favor with me.

Everybody likes six-year-old Gracie. She is highly favored, because she is so mature and self-controlled. As I write, just ten minutes ago I drove past the garden and saw Gracie picking tomatoes while baby-sitting her 20-month-old brother Parker. It is 95 degrees outside with high humidity and she was not just picking tomatoes for lunch; she was picking a bushel to be used in canning. She likes to work! The last I saw of her she had loaded the tomatoes on a golf cart, strapped Parker in, and was driving across the field back to her house. Who wouldn't favor such a child? She is worth more than any three average adults when it comes to completing a job responsibly.

Lazy adults are made out of lazy kids. There is no such thing as a lazy child that grows up to be a diligent adult. Habits formed before a child is ten years old are fixed in the psyche. There is just something ugly about a lazy man. "As vinegar to the teeth, and as smoke to the eyes, so is the sluggard to them that send him" (Proverbs 10:26). They didn't call Solomon wise for nothing.

The Apostle Paul didn't favor lazy men either. There must have been a few of them around in the first century, for he found it necessary to remind the Thessalonian church, "For even when we were with you, this we commanded you, that if any would not work, neither should he eat" (2 Thessalonians 3:10). That's narrow minded—no work, no eat. Get a job or starve. Can't get a job, make one.

Paul also reminded fellow minister, Timothy, "But if any provide not for his own, and specially for those of his own house, he hath denied the faith, and is worse than an infidel" (1 Timothy 5:8). Wow! If a man does not provide for his family, he is denying the faith he professes and is worse than a rank unbeliever.

But of all the Biblical writers speaking against laziness, Jesus was the most negative, saying a slothful man should lose his possessions and be cast into outer darkness.

Matthew 25:26–30:

26 His lord answered and said unto him, Thou wicked and slothful servant, thou knewest that I reap where I sowed not, and gather where I have not strawed:

27 Thou oughtest therefore to have put my money to the exchangers, and then at my coming I should have received mine own with usury.

28 Take therefore the talent from him, and give it unto him, which hath ten talents.

29 For unto every one that hath shall be given, and he shall have abundance: but from him that hath not shall be taken away even that which he hath.

30 And cast ye the unprofitable servant into outer darkness: there shall be weeping and gnashing of teeth.

At what point do you expect a developing human being to become diligent? Diligence is not a job function that one performs because his employer requires it; it is a character trait. It is righteousness. "Whatsoever thy hand findeth to do, do it with thy might; for there is no work, nor device, nor knowledge, nor wisdom, in the grave, whither thou goest" (Ecclesiastes 9:10). A man should conduct his work "not with eye service, as men pleasers; but in singleness of heart, fearing God: And whatsoever ye do, do it heartily, as to the Lord, and not unto men" (Colossians 3:22–23). As you can see, God takes this issue quite seriously. Laziness is depravity resting in nothingness, settling for little while desiring much, with a whole catalogue of excuses. When challenged to go out and find gainful employment, "The slothful man saith, There is a lion without, I shall be slain in the streets" (Proverbs 21:13).

I know sons who cannot get on with their life, cannot consider marriage, because they must take care of their parents. Daddy is too lazy to work. I have heard girls say, "I am not interested in him and won't be until he cuts the strings with his parents."

28-Year-Old Baby

Years ago, a man and his wife came to me concerned for their 28-year-old son who still lived at home and didn't have a job. "What can we do?" they pleaded. Now, I knew the family very well, so I said, "I will tell you how to cure him, but you won't do it."

"Please tell us anyway."

"Kick him out of the house and do not give him any money," I said. Understand, the young man was a good friend of mine. My answer sprung from my concern to see him grow up and take responsibility. The father nodded his agreement and the mother took two steps back like I had told her she should poison her son. "Oh, no," she said, "I couldn't do that, he's my baby."

"That's obvious," said I. "I knew you wouldn't take my advice; that is why he is 28 and still living at home with no females interested in him." He continued to live there for several years and remained immature.

Thankfulness

One character trait God highly favors is thankfulness. "Surely the righteous shall give thanks unto thy name: the upright shall dwell in thy presence" (Psalm 140:13). Children develop thankfulness or the lack thereof through example, parental or otherwise. If you raise your children with a sense of entitlement, they will expect a higher level of personal recognition and privilege. In other words, the threshold at which they feel someone has given them more than they deserve is much higher than the average person. I heard a most humorous remark the other day. When the name of another man came up in conversation, an old country fellow standing by ironically uttered, "I wish I could buy him for what he's worth and sell him for what he thinks he's worth." Everybody dislikes a man, woman, or child that thinks they're worth more than they are.

God is also highly offended by unthankfulness, placing it in the list of sins that will be prominent in the last days. "For men shall be lovers of their own selves, covetous, boasters, proud, blasphemers, disobedient to parents, unthankful, unholy...from such turn away" (2 Timothy 3:2, 5). Note the link from "disobedient to parents" to "unthankful."

It is common knowledge that children raised in wealth are often unthankful. I once had a friend who really valued name brands. Cars, clothes, food, basically everything had to have a special name or it was considered "trash". There was an elderly lady in the church at that time who was seriously naive. She was gentle, kind, loving, and ready to give you her last meal. To her, name brand items were just a way to steal people's money and promote vanity. I look

166

back and see that the old lady had more wisdom than all us young folks put together. The lady often came to church with a "bag of goodies" for different families. She was especially generous to families who had several children and a dad who didn't work regularly, which happened to fit my "name brand" friend to the T. Where the rest of us men beat the bushes for work, he "depended on God" to provide for his family because, as he said, HE ministered. I was careful never to give the lazy bum a dime, but Mrs. Naïve always overlooked his spiritual nonsense and was ready to help out every time she got a good buy on something she knew the family could use.

One Sunday we had a potluck, and Mrs. Naïve brought extra casseroles for the "Name Brand" family so they could stay over. She also had another big box for them, this time it was of used school stuff, books, colored pencils and the like. I heard her ask one of the Name Brand little girls how they liked all the dress up stuff she had given them a few weeks earlier. The child's answer fell on the group of listeners like a boulder. "Oh, Dad opened the box and said it was all trash so he threw it in the garbage. Besides, Daddy says the stuff was used and might be unclean so he didn't want us to touch any of it."

Mrs. Naïve's hand flew to her mouth and her sad, embarrassed eyes glanced around as we all, as one, turned and tried to look as if we didn't hear. Her voice was weak as she asked, "But what about the money I taped to the bottom of the box?" Her kind old voice trailed away as she registered the lack of knowledge in the child's eyes.

Dogs come in all colors, shapes and sizes, and it doesn't make much difference whether they are dressed in name brand or Walmart bargains. The children were being taught unthankfulness, to judge the gift by its quality rather than the intent of the giver.

He could have taught from the Bible every evening and his children would still have been spoiled with unthankfulness.

Teaching Thankfulness

Teach your children to be thankful by example and then by arranging home life so they must earn access to the pleasurable extras of life. They must see the link between labor and reward, between things and the cost. Literature abounds with stories of kings or wealthy men placing their sons as servants or as common men in order to prepare them for the high level of responsibility they will eventually inherit. It is well known that the coddled are not as competent in positions of responsibility than are those who worked their way to the top.

If children do not see the connection between what you provide and their consumption, they will not be appreciative. Certain things we take for granted depending on our culture and life style. In America the only child that has ever thanked his parents for his mattress is the one who had to sleep on the floor for a period of time. I am not suggesting you have your children sleep on the floor; just consider the principle. When I stayed in the Maya Indian village in Central America, one of the guys gave his foam mattress to a man and his wife who knew nothing but sleeping on a wooden bench. They were overjoyed with thankfulness. A kid who never gets candy is very thankful for one piece, but a child that is given unhindered access to junk food assumes that it is his right and is never thankful for a gift of candy. In short, overindulged children never learn to be thankful. You will do well if you take care to establish a connection between the things your children receive and the labor required obtaining it.

Remind your children how hard their father works to provide for them. When they are foolish with their things remind them, "Daddy had to work 12 hours in the hot sun so we could buy this item, so we need to be wise and not waste Daddy's labor."

Economics 101

When our children were growing up, I maintained an economic system for them. They were not remunerated for daily family chores. You live here; you contribute. But if they helped me do something for which I was being paid, they got a share. After moving to the country, I contracted with a company to cut hickory poles to be used in the construction of primitive furniture. They paid $2.25 for each ten-foot pole that was around two inches at the base. The two boys and I could cut, haul out of the woods, and load about 200 poles on a good day. We worked three days a week and hauled the other two, bringing in about six to eight hundred dollars a week. I gave Gabriel seven percent of the haul and Nathan received five percent. We had one of their friends work with us some and he received three percent. That came to about $50 each week for Gabriel and $30 for Nathan. That is the way we made a living for several years. The cutting season only lasted about four months during the fall and winter, so we had to work extremely hard and fast since it wasn't year round work.

The boys were very diligent in work because they saw the connection between every pole cut and their pay at the end of the week. They would ride with me to deliver the poles and on the way home we stopped to eat. They paid for their own meals. When I paid for the meals they wanted a double stacker cheeseburger, fries, milkshake, and cookies. When they had to pay for their meal they only wanted one kiddy burger and water to drink. If I then purchased a large fry and let them split it, they were very thankful.

One summer I contracted to build a barn for a fellow. The boys helped cut pine logs off his land, haul them home, saw them into the appropriate lumber on our mill, and then haul the lumber back to build the barn. Again, they got a percentage of the pay. They worked like little animals, knowing that the sooner we got it finished the more they would make per hour. It's Economics 101 learned in a practical way.

Flea Market Education

We lived far from any shopping center, and seldom got out other than to work. But about once a year we traveled three hours to a big flea market. It covered around 100 acres and was just too big to see in one day. I remember the kids saving up for the shopping trip when they were very young.

Every day they would count their money. Each of them had somewhere between $20 and $45. They were excited—all the possibilities! As we got out of the truck, I told them to not buy until they had checked the entire sale and found the best price. They already knew how to dicker for a lower price, having watched Deb and I do it a hundred times. I crossed paths with them from time to time and slowly they filled their totes with their purchases. Late in the day, our money gone and our purchases stowed, we headed home. On the way home they excitedly told their stories of getting a better price or of finding "just what I always wanted."

But they were soon to learn one of their greatest economic lessons. Just because it was on sale, and just because you got it even cheaper, and just because you always wanted it, doesn't mean you should have purchased it. Over the coming days as I observed them handling their new purchases and listening to little remarks, I noted they all questioned some if not all of their purchases. I think they enjoyed counting the money every day more than they did the use of the items. Rebekah now had a fancy lead rope for her pony, but the eight dollars was gone forever. Rebekah mentioned that the old piece of dirty rope had worked just as well.

I felt their loss. It was sad to see their regret, but I knew it was a lesson well learned. I wouldn't have prevented it for anything. After that experience they were all as tight as a knot in barbed wire. When Nanny and Daddy Bill came to visit and brought the kids something they would have bought if they had been less tight with their money, they were highly grateful, expressing their thanks profusely.

Teach your children to be thankful and they will gain favor with man.

SEVEN

PRACTICAL SUGGESTIONS:

Since you are reading this book and have come nearly to the end, I must assume that you want your children to be strong in spirit and wise, filled with the grace of God, and in favor with God and man.

Teach your children to endure the pain of work and duty. Doing one's duty is noble and brave, requiring sacrifices that can only be performed by a person of character and self-discipline.

It is never too young to start conditioning your children to take responsibility for their actions. Create an environment for children that emulates the real world. Their world must make demands upon them, and there must be real consequences for their actions. I am going to simplify the process and reduce it to eight steps. You will need to use wisdom to flesh it out.

1. First, you must not give your children any occasion to doubt your devotion to their welfare.

If they see you as selfish and duplicitous, if they know you to be lazy while demanding they work, they will relate to you as a slave does to his master—not very constructively. The foundation of all child training is example. Children are rooted in your soul and the fruit will be like the root.

Many parents think they can make everything right by just saying, "I am sorry," but it's not so. I know a woman who loved her children fiercely and did everything she could for them, but she was a basketcase of conflicting emotions, sometimes attending psychological therapy. The psychologists called her bipolar, and from time to time the other pole of her soul would all but curse her children. They were hurt, but she would soon beg their forgiveness, explaining that she didn't mean it and the devil made her do it. But today the kids are gone and she is alone. They never come to see her and "hate her guts." "Sorry" didn't make it right. Today they all agree she is sorry.

This first point is an entirely negative one. It is about what not to do. Do not give your children a single occasion to doubt your devotion and good will toward them. "Sorry" does not undo a deep wound. The following is the positive.

2. You must maintain fellowship with your children.

If they know you enjoy them, they will enjoy being enjoyed and take extra precaution not to jeopardize their primary source of good feelings. We like to please people that are pleased with us. We avoid people that we cannot please. And if we care to please them and have met with repeated failure, we come to hate them for the pain they give us. That is the sad story of most homes.

As a ministry, I have taken children into my home that I do not favor and treated them as my favorite person. I noted one thing they did that pleased me and praised them for it, ignoring the things that displeased me. Within 24 hours of building fellowship with the children, they begin seeking ways to please me. When a cantankerous child or a lazy child taps into the fountain of sweet fellowship, he wants to abide there and will change his behavior to match your expectations. In other words, treat children like you would treat them if they were all you wanted them to be, and they will become that person so as to secure their position in your favor.

There are exceptions to a speedy turnaround. Some kids are so hurt and suspicious that they expect to be manipulated by people trying to "game" them. Such a damaged child will hold out and even test your love by deliberately violating the principle of fellowship, expecting you to turn on them, confirming their opinion of the hypocrisy of authority, allowing them to continue in their troubled world of rebellion. With such a child it takes longer than 24 hours, but if you can ever get them to believe in your love and good will and enjoy the fruit of the relationship, they will make personal sacrifices to maintain the valued relationship.

If there has been a history of hurt and you want to start over with your children, you must first create a new history of joy and blessing. If you spread sunshine with smiles and praise, you will dispel the darkness in your child's soul.

3. You must hold your child's attention.

This is a subtle one and hard to do in our modern digital age. The foundation of all teaching and training, whether in the military, a business seminar, or training an animal, is to hold their attention. If you provide your children with a busy world where their social needs can be met without you, they may just choose other friends that are not so "old fogey" and develop in a different direction as dictated by their social circle.

The person who feeds an animal is the one who trains it. If you are going to be their primary example you must be their benefactor. In short, they must need you. But your duty (and it is a time consuming one) is to be there not just with quality time but with quantity time as well. Parents say, "But I don't have time to be there training my children." Well, you shouldn't have had children then. Why keep a horse if you are not going to take time to train it? They will get trained and they will find someone to be their mentor. You can't just put a child on hold, suspending their development until you have time for them. They are growing fast, and every day is a day of molding into the person they will become. If you are successful in business and are able to provide all the physical things they need, you will not gain their favor, nor they yours. Relationships are built by relating, and relating fills up a calendar.

You hold a child's attention when you are interesting, when your life is interesting, when your relationship to your spouse is interesting, when your relationship to God is interesting.

You hold a child's attention when you are a source of intellectual development. If you are intellectually boring, you will not find favor with an enquiring mind. If you are not learning, you cannot share new ideas.

You hold a child's attention when you are spiritually challenging. If your relationship to God is routine, your religion will be easy to dismiss as shallow and meaningless. But if you are actively praying, studying, and sharing your faith, you will be a challenge to your children. Volleyball players don't enjoy playing ball with players who are not challenging. If they cannot run them off, they will pack up and leave the court to the amateurs.

When you have their attention, you can be certain they are developing parallel to you. Your soul becomes the source of their worldview.

4. You must live an ordered, responsible, and productive life, and include your children as vital participants.

If you would instill order and productivity in your children you must begin when they are born. Kids who grow up in the South eating field peas and okra think it is the best food in the world, but people from Wisconsin think rhubarb pie is a treat. Personally, I think it's a poor substitute for an apple. I wouldn't feed it to the chickens, but then a Southern chicken wouldn't eat it anyway. I have friends who think chittlins are great, but I won't get in the same room with pig guts on a platter. It is all in how you are raised.

What you provide by way of order and responsibility when they are young will establish their expectations and set their habits for the rest of their lives. You cannot demand something of your children that you do not live and do not provide.

I once had a man working for me that was a man of character and his children followed in his footsteps, exemplary in every way, except one: neatness. I would send him to organize and clean up a mess and when finished I couldn't tell much difference. Now I am messy as well. When I get to doing a job I never look back at the destruction I am leaving behind. My wife says it is more work for her when I cook than if she did it herself, because of the mess I make. Women seem to clean up as they go along. Some of us men need a full time cleaning crew to follow us.

There were times I sent this man to clean up the same spot three times and it still needed cleaning. His perception of clean is just different from the average person.

Later I hired his son to work for me. The boy had great work ethic—best helper I ever had. He was not afraid of work or long hours, but he was afraid of clean and neat. Like his daddy, he would walk off and leave tools exposed to the weather. When I gave him a cleanup job, he would sweep out the middle of the floor but not the corners. In the yard he would pick up the obvious trash but not out-of-the-way garbage. I could tell he thought cleanup was a big waste of time. Like father, like son.

There are many things a lot worse to pass on to your kids, but I want you to see the principle. Kids are what you make them to be.

5. You must be clear in defining the rules that govern family life.

Clearly define the day-to-day housekeeping and social rules, things we should do for the sake of courtesy and harmony in relating to one another. Character and lifelong habits are formed in those early years by the structure imposed on the family.

We humans are a living soul in a body of flesh. It is a fire and water mixture, two opposite elements that cannot mix. Children come into the world with flesh that is totally untrained and ready to indulge to the fullest, while their souls lack the maturity to be self-determinate. [See my book *By Divine Design*.] Rules are not natural to children. They don't like them. Rules at any age are limitations upon actions, imposed upon the soul as a duty to be obeyed. If a rule is to be obeyed, the soul must choose to deny the body its unrestrained gratification. Thus the conflict will always result in the soul surrendering to the appetite unless the flesh is trained to suffer the pain and deprivation of choosing the good for the good's sake. Wow!

We parents have a big job. It reminds me of the fat, lazy man trying to teach his wife to be temperate and exercise. We parents should live the high moral ground when it comes to training our children to walk after the spirit rather than the flesh. If you want more on this subject get my audio series, *Body, Soul, and Spirit*.

Given the nature of a child we can understand Solomon's observation, "A child left to himself bringeth his mother to shame" (Proverbs 29:15). Children will resist every rule, they will buck authority, they will rebel against the rule of law, and they will do so with an increasing understanding of ways to manipulate their parents to feel badly for making such "unreasonable" demands upon them. They will lie to you that they are hungry, that they are cold or in pain, all for a little attention. "They go astray as soon as they be born, speaking lies" (Psalm 58:3). Like you, I sometimes give in to them. They are not smarter than I am, but they don't need to be when I am so ready to be used in a manner that satisfies my own need to be needed.

But the day of reckoning comes quickly. Before their first year they have developed enough understanding to scream the language of indulgence. There comes a point when they stop meeting our need to be needed and start irritating us with their unfounded protests. At that point we start wondering if we are up to the task of parenting—beaten by an eight-month-old. We either train or they remain indulgent and hedonistic.

The most common problem is that parents react instead of becoming proactive. Reactions are tit for tat and never produce anything other than more reactions until the reactor melts down and the kid leaves home screaming, "I hate you."

The solution: become a trainer instead of a complainer. "Train up a child in the way he should go: and when he is old, he will not depart from it" (Proverbs 22:6). If you have not already read *To Train Up A Child* now is the time to do so. I will not revisit training in detail here since I have done so in several other books, but a restatement of the principle and method is in order.

You train children by example, persuasion, and constraint—in that order.

All three methods will be employed on any given day, and none of them are effective unless all three are in place at the same time. Without furnishing your children with a good example of self-constraint, self-discipline, and self-denial, persuasion will fall on deaf ears and be met with sounds of dissent. Constraint will be met with anger and resentment.

If you provide good example and you constrain them to obedience but fail to use persuasion, your children will be confused and feel unloved. Persuasion is called reproof in the Bible. "The rod and reproof give wisdom...." (Proverbs 29:15). Reproof or persuasion is where you instruct the child as to the reasons he should obey.

And, of course, constraint without proper example and persuasion is cruel and totally ineffective other than breaking the spirit of your child.

Modern left wing liberal parents who have been psyched out of their common sense, having given up traditional family training methods, believe in example and persuasion but do not hold with constraint. There has never been a society, a city, or even a small village that has survived without the threat and reality of constraint. Where there is no constraint there is no law. Where there is no law there is lawlessness. It is foolish idealism to think you can love children into self-disciplined lives. If they did not have bodies filled with passions to indulge, it would be possible to persuade a child to right acting, but reality being reality, the only effective approach to child training is example first, then persuasion backed up by the certainty of constraining force. Spankless parents produce thankless kids.

The proof is empirical. I could introduce you to millions of families that have outstanding results producing creative, self-disciplined, happy adults by means of their example followed by persuasion and backed up by measured constraint. To read hundreds of examples of parents applying this method, read the books *No Greater Joy* Volumes 1-3.

6. Teach them God's Rules.

Training children to obey the rules is vital, but their training must go further if you want them to find favor with God. "Let not mercy and truth forsake thee: bind them about thy neck; write them upon the table of thine heart: So shalt thou find favour and good understanding in the sight of God and man" (Proverbs 3:3–4). God favors those who love his Word, who walk in righteousness, and seek him with their whole heart. While we are training our children to honor household and family rules, we should also be communicating God's rules. When a child lies they should be spanked, but they should also be admonished as to the evils of being a liar, and when they are of sufficient age and understanding we should inform them of God's judgment upon liars. The same holds true with all moral precepts—anger, violence, bitterness, gossip, hate, jealousy, lust, laziness, intemperance, evil talk, and much more.

Now here is the key: Children should know that just as the home is under the rule of law, governed by the certainty of constraint, so life in general is governed by God's rule of law with the certainty of a day of judgment. Under your governorship, as they come to understand that all actions have consequences, they will make that transfer to God's government, knowing that God's judgments are as certain as yours. That is the power you have as the lawgiver and enforcer. You model God's kingdom and set the stage for your children to surrender to his rule in their lives.

Just as you model the government of God, you must also model the grace of God. Your entire home-life is a visual aid in teaching your children Divine reality. They must understand and appreciate law and judgment, but they should graduate to grace and mercy. There is no grace without law and there is no mercy without guilt. The law will uncover their transgression and mete out punishment, but then grace forgives and clears away all indebtedness, leaving the child purged from guilt and renewed to try again.

After disciplining a child, you should restore him to fellowship. Remember, the greatest persuasion you have is the power of fellowship. Your children should see that the chastisement you mete out, be it spanking or something else, has been effective in satisfying the demands of justice. Remember, you are modeling God's relationship to us. He is a God of law and justice, but he is also a God of grace and forgiveness. If you are weak on the grace, you will leave them under the bondage of the law and it will either crush them or make them rebellious.

7. Provide your children with a hopeful vision.

A tough trail can be endured for the reward that lies at the end of it. Children are more full of life than are we. They are romantic and expect great things. If we do not provide an obvious avenue to the fulfilling of their vision for the future they will jump ship on us, leaving the home prematurely in anger. See my book *Jumping Ship*.

Children will fully develop when they see the path forward and value it. Provide them with a community life that promises a future spouse, a vocation, opportunity to learn the skills they will need to excel. When they have hope they will hang in there during times of confusion or temptation. They should believe that you will do all you can to launch them into the world as adults. Their spirits will soar with bright hope and anticipation.

All parents have great aspirations for their children. The difference is in whether we are willing to pay the price to make it happen. Go thou and do likewise.

My String Of Pearls

I asked each of our children to write on a particular memory or subject. This is a reflection of how they view their life.

Shalom

When I was a little girl, my sister and I played house all day, every day. We would build our play pretend houses everywhere we went. I remember days when Dad would come from work and stop in shock at the mess Shoshanna and I had made in the sunroom. We would take every book, chair, cushion, cardboard, or blanket that mom would let us use and build ourselves a fancy home.

One time we found a pile of old flowers the graveyard keeper had tossed over the fence onto our farm. In great excitement, we took them to our yard and stuck them into the ground to create flower walls for our house. We thought it was so wonderful. We ran to find Dad and Mom so they could come and see our wonderful new house. With great pleasure and pride we showed it off. Like the fine parents they are, they smiled and sat at a makeshift table in our magnificent flower kitchen room and pretended to eat with us.

I look back to my childhood and realize that when my parents saw the plastic flowers all over the front lawn they must have been thinking, "Oh No! What a mess!" But as a child I never had a clue that our flower playhouse was anything but beautiful. Their smart little girls only filled their hearts with gladness.

The first year of my marriage I lived in a magical world of making a real house become a special home. A pleasure and pride, very akin to what I knew as a child, daily filled my heart. When Dad and Mom came over to visit, I fed them real food at a real table, and it was so much fun.

Last night my good husband brought home some short pieces of wood from his job. My two little girls found it, and right now, as I am writing this, both are outside gleefully making a new playhouse with the small pieces of wood and some fake flowers left over from a party. When they are finished making their playhouse, like my mother before me, I will go out and sit with them in their kitchen and pretend to eat dirt cake. And someday, when my daughters are married, with the same pride that they once fed me dirt cake they will feed me fine foods at their real table. They will, as I have done, reflect back to the glorious days of their childhood, remembering that Mama took time to play pretend with them.

Last evening Gracie asked, "Mom, why are you such a good mom?"

I answered her question with a question. "Who is my mama?

Laila, my four-year-old daughter, exclaimed, "Mama Pearl."

I smiled as I answered, knowing that they were already seeing the truth I wished to convey. "That's right, and what kind of mama is she?"

Gracie's voice was full of wisdom as she replied, "I know! She is the best Mama Pearl in the whole wide world, and she was your mama and taught you how to be a good mama. That's right, isn't it Mama?"

I smiled and said, "Yes, that's right, and someday you will be the best mama in the whole wide world."

My mama trained me by letting me practice being a mama. By appreciating our playhouses and graciously allowing us to play hostess to her and Dad, they were teaching my sister and me to be happy wives and mothers. I was raised on joy. My children are being trained with the same spirit.

Rebekah

(From Mike)

Just as I was finishing up this book Deb and I went out west to spend some time with our out west grandkids. Since our daughter Rebekah knows that I do not like to just sit and do nothing, she had some chores for us to do while we were there. Joe, the grandson you will read about in the following article, now stands tall and strong, just a few short years from manhood. He climbs a rope hand over hand with little thought or effort. While Deb worked with our granddaughters butchering chickens for the freezer, Joe and I worked as a team building a new chicken house and fence. When we finished there, we went to his grandparents' old log cabin to do some repair work. I have learned my lesson about climbing to high places, so Joe did all the high work as I stood in the shade and advised. We refurbished the old screen door and a few other things around the old home place. He found great joy in doing this service for his grandparents whom he loves so much, while I found great pleasure in seeing his strong body, willingness to work, and kind heart.

Rebekah is our oldest child. She, like her mama and daddy, is a writer. But there are seasons in everyone's life. Now Rebekah is in full swing of the "being a wife and a mama" season. Before she married she was a linguist working in the mountains of Papua New Guinea with a tribe so remote that they had never before seen a white person. When Beka came back home she told us about hairy spiders so heavy (about the size of a man's hand) that when they dropped from the ceiling they landed with a thud that would wake you up at night—with no lights to turn on, that would terrify even ME. Sometimes they landed on the bed, even her face. SPLAT! Scary.

When my mother-in-law heard stories like that she always said, "Well, her mama sure didn't raise no sissies." Our son Gabriel went with Beka for her first few months as a linguist. When the tiny mountain folks saw his strapping 6'6" frame they called him "Walking Tree." Beka kept a diary while she lived and worked there with the unwritten language. Her diary was so intriguing we decided to share it with others. It's simply called *Rebekah's Diary*. Nowadays her ministry is training up some of the finest children you will ever meet. They play the piano and violin and are excelling in their home education.

When I told her we wanted her to write an article for this book dealing with homeschooling she replied that the article had already been written, now she was living it. So this story goes back to when Joe was just two years old and their family was just budding.

Rebekah

Beginning with Words

For weeks now, my two-year-old has had the obnoxious habit of repeating himself over and over. At first I continued to answer him patiently—the same answer ten times in a row. Next I resorted to ignoring him; but the questioning went on. Finally, I threatened to spank him if he kept asking the same question after he had received the answer. Then one day, he asked me a question that did not need an answer—and then asked it again in a different way. "I see no stars up there, Mom?" "Mom, do I see no stars up there?"

A light went on in my brain. I began to recall my own experiences with language learning in Papua New Guinea [her missionary story is found in her book, Rebekah's Diary]. Could my two-year-old possibly be cognizant enough to be learning his first language in such a structured manner? So, for the first time, instead of answering his question, "I don't know whether you see any stars or not, Joe," I repeated his phrase back to him with the proper grammar. "I don't see any stars up there, Mom." He looked at me with absolute delight and jumped up and down yelling, "I don't see any stars up there, Mom!" The next few days were an intense learning session. Joseph's ability to talk grew by leaps and bounds. He questioned me continually; and now, instead of answering what had appeared as dumb questions, I would carefully articulate the grammar and phonetics of a whole exchange for him. He repeated each phrase until he could say it all properly without coaching.

Joe: "You got to wash a dishes, Mom?"

Mom: "Do you need to wash the dishes, Mom?"

Joe: "Do you need to wash the dishes, Mom?"

Mom: "Yes, Joseph, I need to wash the dishes. Would you like to help me?"

Joe: "Like to help me?"

Mom: "I want to help you, Mom."

Joe: "I want to help you, Mom."

His affection for me became hilariously dear. We were close before, but now we had become best buddies in just a few hours. I was suddenly the only person in the world who could tell him exactly what he wanted to know.

My curiosity was aroused; did all toddlers face this problem? I began to listen in Walmart and the bank when I went to town. What I heard was different levels of understanding. Some children seemed to be under the impression that there wasn't necessarily a correct way to speak. Perhaps that was because the adults in their lives simply repeated their baby talk back to them, thinking it cute. Other children had obviously discovered the truth and were in various stages of learning with their oblivious teachers. I can sympathize with these kids in their efforts to learn a language from a clueless adult.

I spent two years among the Kumboi people of Papua New Guinea. Most of that time involved linguistics and translation. I squatted for hours in the smoke filled cookhouse in the center of our village practicing the words I learned and trying to pick up new ones. The villagers loved to hear me talk. It amused them to hear a grown person falter and slur words just like their toddlers. I encountered the same problem Joseph often does when my Kumboi friends failed to correctly repeat my words. Their first response was to say them the same poor way I had because it was funny.

Among my friends was a young married girl from one of the most remote and uncivilized villages in the region. She was often teased for forgetting to wear a shirt or comb the debris out of her hair in the morning. Natalin did not speak the trade language at all when I first came and was confined to the local tribal language alone. Natalin was my favorite language helper. She was a natural teacher. When I said a word incorrectly, Natalin did not think it was funny; she must have understood the frustration of not being able to communicate. Her response to me was always swift and loud. With perfect enunciation and tones, Natalin would repeat the desired word or phrase for me the way it should be said. Even today, seven years later, I can hear her voice ringing in my head. She would bob her head at me, directing me to keep repeating to her until I said the phrase to her satisfaction. Next this unlearned but brilliant teacher would pick up an object on the dirt floor and begin an instructive conversation in which I would have to use my new phrase correctly.

Natalin made me excited about learning a language. Her focus was never on my inabilities, but rather on the task at hand. I not only learned Kumboi from Natalin; I learned how to teach as well. Like every good mother, I tend to think my child is exceptional. I imagine him orating to thousands and amazing them with his eloquence. But this week has been enlightening for me. I look at little children with different eyes—or I should say, I hear them with different ears!

Long before our children begin "school" they are developing a propensity to learn. If that desire to learn is thwarted or denied, it might wither and die. If it is cultivated and cared for, it will doubtless grow. I have often said that homeschooling is a way of life, not just a way of learning. Now I believe that teaching is a way of life as well.

Nathan

As I read through this book, laughing with pleasure at all the things we did when we were children, I couldn't help but think of critics over the years lamenting at the awful childhood we children must have had, how we must be weak of spirit, broken, sad, and unable to perform in life. What a wonderful childhood we had! I would just like to say to Dad, "Thanks." Thanks for putting us first. Thanks for taking the time to take us fishing, to take us hunting, to make us work, teaching us self-discipline, teaching us how to build a sawmill, and, yes, for teaching us to believe in ourselves. Thanks for putting your family first, first by example and then by teaching the Word of God. Thanks for giving us a foundation that enables us to live in harmony within our families.

As I read this book to my children I recalled the many things I have been privileged to do. I can fly an airplane, climb a mountain, rappel, swim in various adverse conditions, scuba dive, and study the Bible and anything else I choose to learn with clarity and understanding. I've traveled a big part of the globe, visiting and even living in some of the most remote and beautiful regions: Asia, the South Pacific, Central America, and more. For over a decade I've run my own business.

And above all, of the many people I have met, I know I have the best relationship with my wife, bar none. None of that would be possible without the foundation you read here in this book as well as Dad's first book, *To Train Up A Child.*

Critics of Biblically-based, traditional training say my upbringing was not normal. I agree. I am glad we are not normal. I am glad we have a father who is radical enough to put us first, radical enough to lay aside plans deeming his family more important, radical enough to do the right things even when it is not popular.

In my business, I worked with a man who was on the road 25 days a month. He told me that because he couldn't be at home he bought his kids really nice things and spent quality time with them. I am very glad that was not my father's plan. He helped us make things instead of buying them, and even better than that, he gave us the confidence to make our own things. He gave us the ability and know-how to do and be whatever we want. Not because of wealth or privilege, but because of strength of spirit and body. So to the critic, the reason that you don't understand this kind of upbringing and family is because you have been left out. If you only knew.

Gabriel

I spent these past few evenings between dinner and playing with the kids reading my parents' new book. It gave me a refreshing look back at my early life. After thinking about it, one of the things I believe is most important is that raising children strong in spirit is not limited to one particular life style or region. Whether you are a missionary in Mongolia, a farmer in California, or a painter in Atlanta, here are some of the forks in the road I'm thankful my parents took.

Even though my dad didn't have the time or will to take me hunting twice a day as a young child, he allowed me to go. With well-defined and enforced safety perimeters, he understood that even a six- or seven-year-old needs to roam free sometimes. When I was eight or nine he allowed us to go fishing with some of the trusted brothers in our church. Yes, I would have been happy to stay home with Mama, but I wouldn't have been the same person today. When I was ten, baseball came along. My dad never played sports, his free throw average was around three percent, but he did not force me to do what he liked, he let me play baseball. He set up a pitching mound at home and encouraged me to practice, even spending time trying to teach what he knew, which was not very much. He went to the games and rooted for us. My brother and I only played one year. Other things were more interesting, but it was just another part of our education.

The soil that nourished us as young plants was definitely my mom. She was always there to support us. She not only took me to the Goodwill to find an old baseball glove, but she helped give me the confidence that I could do it.

By the time I was 16 or 17, I camped 60 days out of the year. Being free to do that provided me with a healthy

outlet to burn off a lot of the energy that makes teenagers a pain. So keep it fun, keep it light, keep it wholesome and real. And whatever you do, keep your kids away from video games.

Pushing, steering, and allowing us to explore our interests at an early age caused all of us children to develop a love for learning. I highly recommend this book. The stories are real life events. I lived them.

Shoshanna

This week I read Dad's new book to my husband and five year old son, Jeremiah. We laughed and learned things new and things forgotten. Jeremiah was so excited to hear all the stories of my childhood. It was awesome to see the things I learned growing up through my son's eyes. It was like looking at myself when I was five. The thrill of recognizing danger and knowing how to avoid it was a big thing in my life. From my earliest memories, learning that wisdom was mine simply for the asking was a heady, glorious thing. I have always loved the excitement of rising to the challenges of life. Another biggie for me is the security that comes in knowing that the God that made Heaven and Earth is always watching over me with good will. I have always felt his smile and blessing.

As far back as I can remember I have been proud that my parents are proud of me. That sense of their approval has made me bold, confident, capable, and ready for anything. I grew up feeling that I was a queen, but was trained to love serving everyone. I was just a girl, but I knew I could beat Tarzan flying through the jungle. I was determined, strong willed, and graceful. My daddy made me feel that way. As I read Dad's stories to my son, I couldn't resist looking into his face. I could see his chest rising and his eyebrows sharpening. I saw the pride in my son's eyes that I am his mama. When I read what his Big Papa wrote about him, it was like watching a male peacock letting you know he was "The Man". Jeremiah's heart is big, his imagination wild, and his confidence is off the radar. I knew my son was feeling the same sense of value I always felt. It is good, very good.

Children are so much fun! Marriage is so much fun! Life is so much better having each other, making each other better, living life unselfishly for one another. My parents raised us first and foremost by showing us what men and women should be. They were our examples of love, marriage, family, courage, strength, honor, compassion, kindness, wisdom, happiness, and a desire to love God with all their heart, mind, and soul. They were our examples. You are your children's example. Everything you do, everything you say, what you eat, who you

Joe Courage (5) is learning to read...

hang out with, and those with whom you allow them to hang out. You are their example.

I am married to an awesome man named James. No, he is not always perfect, and neither am I, but that is when we are really tested to show good examples, to love when the other is not so lovable. Our children are watching us, taking cues. Jeremiah James takes loving care of his baby sister Penelope Jane. Sometimes she pulls his hair or pinches him, but he just turns to her and says, "No, no, Penelope! That hurt me. You need to be a sweet girl." That is about the time they start hug wrestling. Watching them I smile to myself, knowing I am doing something right. I was blessed to have good teachers. Now so are you.

I am Shoshanna Rashell Easling, Mike and Debi Pearl's youngest daughter. I am the author of the *Making Babies* DVD series and cookbook. My wonderful husband and I own and run the Bulk Herb Store. Visit us at www.bulkherbstore.com. My final recommendation is that you learn and live well.

Of Utmost Concern

This section was written ten years ago. It's truth is timeless.

I think many of you feel as I do. My most important personal concern has always been my children, and now my many grandchildren command my attention. Even before I was married, my occupation, financial security, ministry, personal fulfillment, all took third place to concerns for my future children. What does "it profit a man if he shall gain the whole world, and lose his own soul?" Likewise, what does it profit a father if he gains the whole world and loses the souls of his children?

What can be called success if your children turn out to be part of the world's problem rather than its cure? What satisfaction can there be in the comforts of material success if your children grow up needing counsel rather than being sought after to give counsel? If your children lie awake at night suffering from guilt and anxiety, being gnawed upon by the demons of intemperance and self-indulgence, how can you enjoy your food or your pillow? The fruit that is borne measures the success of both a tree and a man. The fruit of a man or woman is their children; everything else is falling leaves.

If the sun rises and sets and I never cast a bigger shadow, what of it, if my children are growing and flourishing in God's family? Let me die poor; let me die early; let me be ravaged by disease; just let my children rise up and call me blessed. Let me not measure my giving by the dollars I spend on them or the educational opportunities that my station in life affords, but rather by the hours I spend with them in fellowship.

May they graduate from my tutorship to become disciples of the Man from Nazareth. May they learn good and evil from the pinnacle of obedience rather than from the pit of despair. May they have the wisdom to choose the precious, and the courage to reject the trite and the vain. May they always labor for the meat that endures.

May they be lovers of God, coworkers with the Holy Spirit, and a friend to the Lord Jesus. And when their trail ends, may it end at the throne of God, laying crowns at the Savior's feet.

And that is my prayer for your children as well.

Amen and Amen.

More from Michael and Debi Pearl

Samuel

Sara Sue

To Train Up A Child

Turning the hearts of the fathers to the children. $7.95

Yell & Tell Series

Priceless tools for parents wanting to protect their children. "Those prepared are usually spared." $9.95 each

Free Magazine

No Greater Joy Ministries Inc. publishes a bimonthly magazine with timely articles, stories, etc. Sign up online at www.nogreaterjoy.org or send your name and mailing address to No Greater Joy Ministries, 1000 Pearl Road, Pleasantville, TN 37033. Your information is confidential. We do not share your information with anyone.

For these and other No Greater Joy materials go to NoGreaterJoy.org or call 866-292-9936

Marriage Materials

Created To Be His Help Meet

Learn how to be the wife God created you to be. $14.95

Created To NEED A Help Meet

Unlock the mysterious code to make a wife truly happy. $14.95

Preparing To Be A Help Meet

Preparing for a good marriage begins long before the wedding vows. $19.95

Evangelism and Bible Study

Good and Evil

Your children will grow in wisdom learning the Bible. Now translated into over 30 languages. $24.95

For these and other No Greater Joy materials go to NoGreaterJoy.org or call 866-292-9936